Digital Scrapbook Artist 2
User Guide

How to Contact Us

Our main office
(UK, Europe):

The Software Centre
PO Box 2000, Nottingham,
NG11 7GW, UK

Main:

(0115) 914 2000

Registration (UK only):

(0800) 376 1989

Sales (UK only):

(0800) 376 7070

Customer Service/
Technical Support:

http://www.serif.com/support

General Fax:

(0115) 914 2020

North American office
(USA, Canada):

The Software Center
13 Columbia Drive, Suite 5,
Amherst NH 03031, USA

Main:

(603) 889-8650

Registration:

(800) 794-6876

Sales:

(800) 55-SERIF or 557-3743

Customer Service/
Technical Support:

http://www.serif.com/support

General Fax:

(603) 889-1127

Online

Visit us on the Web at:

http://www.serif.com/

International

Please contact your local distributor/dealer. For further details, please contact
us at one of our phone numbers above.

Table of Contents

Welcome

1

Welcome to Serif Digital Scrapbook Artist!

Serif Digital Scrapbook Artist is the scrapbooking solution that combines scrapbooking fun with a wealth of powerful tools to ensure a fantastic design experience.

Digital Scrapbook Artist comes complete with **DaisyTrail Digikits**, offering themed items that you can use as starting points for your scrapbooks. Each pack includes a selection of **layouts**, **backgrounds**, **embellishments**, **materials**, **photo frames**, and decorative **letters**.

Use the layouts as page templates, then drag and drop items of your choice onto your page. Each Digikit also provides supporting **effects**, **brushes**, and color **swatches** that uniquely complement the theme.

If you're feeling really creative, you can even create and save your own Digikits!

In addition to supplying ready-to-go scrapbook content, Digital Scrapbook Artist lets you add decorative **lines**, **shapes**, and **stencils**. You can also apply natural or spray **brush strokes** using easy-to-use drawing and painting tools. You can add your own photos to your scrapbook, and apply image adjustments and effects using the powerful **PhotoLab**. You can even cut out the subject of a photo, and create your own photo frames!

Once you've created your masterpiece, you'll want to share it. A lively web-based scrapbooking community—**www.daisytrail.com**—is available for you to share your scrapbooks freely or to selected groups. You'll make some new scrapbooking friends along the way too!

Don't forget to visit DaisyTrail.com to download your free Digikits—and purchase new ones!

New features

PhotoLab adjustments

- **Apply non-destructive adjustment filters to your photos**
  PhotoLab provides an impressive selection of editable photo adjustments (**White Balance**, **Lighting**, **Curves**, to name just a few...) and creative effects (including a selection of artistic effects such as **Pencil**, **Watercolor**, and **Oil**).

  You can apply single or multiple filters to an entire photo, or to selected areas using a mask. Your original photo remains intact. You can even save adjustment/effect combinations as **Favorites** for future use.

  PhotoLab also includes **Red-eye** and **Spot-repair** tools for easy retouching. (See *Applying PhotoLab filters* on p. 94.)

Creativity

- **Add impact to your page with a ready-to-go stencil**
  The **Stencils** tab provides a wide selection of ready-to-go stencil templates—designs include birds, people, plants, shapes, and more. The stencils are quick and easy to use, and provide endless opportunities for creativity. Simply drag and drop your chosen stencil onto your page, then paint over it with the **Brush tool**, or use it to cut out a design from a photograph. (See *Using stencils* on p. 203.)

- **Design custom color palettes with Color Palette Designer**
  For quick results, simply pick your base color and then choose from a range of related colors. You can add suggested colors automatically, or mix your own colors to create a new palette. (See *Creating custom palettes* in online Help.)

- **Experiment with the new line control property**
  The **Line** tab's new **Offset** property increases drawing power and

flexibility by letting you adjust the distance between an object and its
outline.

- **Use blend modes to change the way color is applied to your page**
  The Color tab's new blend mode options let you adjust the way in
  which color is applied, giving you more control over the way in
  which items (shapes, brush strokes, photos, etc.) appear on your
  page. (See *Understanding blend modes* in online Help.)

Ease of use

- **Add multiple photos to your page in a single step!**
  Use the new **AutoFlow** feature to automatically populate placed
  photo frames with photos from the **Photos** tab. (See *Using
  AutoFlow* on p. 114.)

- **Find used photos quickly and easily**
  To quickly and easily identify photos used in your scrapbook,
  simply look for those displaying check marks on the **Photos** tab.

- **Convert photos to frameless frames**
  Photos you've added directly to your page (i.e., those that are not
  inside a decorative photo frame) can be converted so that they sit
  inside "frameless" frames. These frames function exactly like the
  decorative frames you've added from the **Frames** tab, allowing you
  to crop, zoom, and pan the photos inside them. You can even use
  the **AutoFlow** feature to automatically replace frame contents! (See
  Converting photos to frames on p. 120.)

- **Add your own Digikit search locations!**
  When you open Scrapbook Artist, it automatically searches to find
  your installed Digikits, so that it can offer them for selection in the
  Digikit Browser. If you want to use Digikits that are stored on
  other **fixed hard drives** or on **removal drives**, you can now add
  these locations to the default search list. (See *Adding Digikit
  locations* in online Help.)

● **Add a mask layer with a single-click!**
Previous versions of Digital Scrapbook Artist allowed you to create mask layers from the **Layer Properties** dialog. Now you can add a new mask layer, or turn an existing layer into a mask, by simply clicking a button on the **Layers** tab! (See *Using masks* in online Help.)

Key features

Scrapbook essentials

● **Themes and Digikits** (p. 17)
Choose just the scrapbook theme you're looking for! Themed Digikits, such as Doll House and Enchanted, are rich in scrapbook items. Your chosen items are loaded into **Content tabs** ready to drag and drop onto the page—nothing could be easier! You can increase the number of themed Digikits available to you with a **Digikit Collection DVD**, or browse the latest Digikit selections on the **www.daisytrail.com** website.

● Use **Digikit Creator** to create and edit your own custom digikits!

● **Scrapbook page sizes** (p. 71)
Design on traditional 8" x 8" or 12" x 12" pages, as well as standard Letter or A4 page formats. Or why not use a custom page size to create your own unique greetings card!

● **Cutting, erasing, and adding to items** (p. 161)
Take your 'virtual' scissors to scrapbook material with the **Scissors tool**—choose from a wide selection of scissor cut types (Square, Pinking, Shark Fin, ZigZag, and more). Use the **Erase** and **Freeform Paint** tools to remove and add to items.

● **Design, print, and upload in high-resolution**
In Digital Scrapbook Artist, 300dpi native working is the norm. All scrapbook items are high-resolution so quality is guaranteed.

Printing and upload at 300dpi gives truly outstanding high-quality output.

Layer work made easy

For greater design control, store scrapbook items on **layers**—work on items on one layer without affecting items on other layers. Layers can be created, merged, and hidden, and display a hierarchical tree view of associated items for easy selection. Apply paper textures to layer items!

Share via website (p. 257)

Upload scrapbooks to Serif's scrapbook community website, **www.daisytrail.com**. View layouts using powerful **zoom** technology, give an **I Love It! rating**, **comment** on, or **search** for any scrapbook by tag. Create public or private **groups** for like-minded scrapbookers—great for making new friends! Take part in scrapbooking discussions in DaisyTrail's **forums**.

Ease of use

Total ease of use

Tabbed, collapsible, and dockable **Studio tabs** are always at hand. Choose from preset colors, line styles, brushes, and effects, or create your own. Use tabs to arrange, transform, and align items.

Context toolbars

Context toolbars offer different tools and options depending on the currently selected item. Great for efficiency and simplifying your workflow. (For details, see online Help.)

Design aids (p. 79)

Rotate your canvas through any angle, just like an artist would do in real life. For more focused design, use **Solo Mode** to work on items in isolation. Use the **Rule of Thirds** tool on your photos or on your scrapbook page for improved page composition.

Photos

- **Adding photos** (p. 83)
  Personalize your scrapbook by **importing your own photos** from hard disk, CD/DVD, digital camera or scanner. Store photos in the **Photos tab** before dragging directly onto a page or into a photo frame.

- **Cropping and fitting photos to frames** (p. 91)
  Use the **Crop Tool** to remove unwanted areas of your photo. For perfect photo placement, you can **scale**, **pan**, and **rotate** photos to your liking.

- **Photo cutouts** (p. 102)
  Cutout Studio makes light work of cutting out your photos. Use brushes to discard backgrounds (sky, walls, etc.) or keep subjects of interest (people, objects, etc.).

- **Create your own photo frames** (p. 121)
  Frame Editor allows you to create your own Digikit photo frames from a photo-based image of a frame.

- Use **QuickFrame**, an ornate QuickShape, to frame your photos.

Brushes

- **Realistic brush strokes** (p. 209)
  Unleash the painter within you with Digital Scrapbook Artist's powerful **Brush tool**! Apply **natural** or **spray** brush strokes using brush types from the Brush tab's galleries—pick brushes chosen from Digikits, pick from preset categories, or create your own. Even apply a brush stroke around item edges!

- **Natural brush strokes**
  The **Natural Media** category hosts **Acrylic**, **Charcoal**, **Paint**, **Felt Tip**, and **Watercolor** brushes. Use **Embroidery** brushes on cut materials, or why not adorn your scrapbook page with lace and ribbon **Photo** brush effects.

- **Spray brush strokes**
  Have fun with **spray brushes** from categories such as **Airbrush**, **Embroidery**, **Flowers**, **Fun & Celebrations**, **Glitter**, and more.

Drawing

- **Design inspiration**
  Use the Online tab to view video tutorials explaining how to use Digital Scrapbook Artist 2's tools and how to apply various creative techniques.

- **QuickShapes** (p. 183)
  QuickShapes work like intelligent clipart which can morph into a myriad of different shape variations. Even extremely complex shapes like spirals, stars, and webs are simple to draw.

- **Copy fills and effects between objects!** (p. 202)
  Use the **Format Painter** to copy fills and effects between objects.

- **Versatile line and curve drawing** (p. 184)
  For natural smooth curves, click and drag with the **Pen tool**, even edit Bezier curve segments with selectable join options. Draw straight or freeform lines with the **Pencil tool**. Join any line's ends to create irregular filled shapes!

- **Artistic and shape text** (p. 125)
  Apply artistic text or text within QuickShapes right on the page... apply basic formatting from the always-at-hand Text context toolbar. Convert text to curves for text design freedom.

- **Color and transparency control** (p 223)
  Apply solid color or transparency to any drawn item's line or fill (or brush stroke) with the Color tab. The tab hosts color **swatches** from Digikits, an HSL color wheel (for custom color selection), and transparency slider. Use the **Fill Tool** to apply gradient, plasma, or mesh fills for exciting results—a gradient fill path lets you add or replace colors and/or transparency simultaneously for more subtle gradients.

- **Filter effects** (p. 147)
  Give your scrapbook items depth with Material Depth or soft edges with Feather Edge. Why not apply drop shadows with the **Shadow Tool** or enliven your text with fully adjustable Inner Shadow, Glow, Bevel, and Emboss filters? All are easy to apply and sure to impress.

- **Astounding 3D lighting and surface effects** (p. 151)
  The Studio's Effects tab offers preset 3D effects (metals, elements, glass, stone, wood, and more) you can apply one or more effects, then customize by varying surface and source light properties.

Sharing

- **Email scrapbook images to friends and family**
  Send your scrapbook as Adobe Acrobat PDF and the popular JPEG format—or simply email your .sbp file!

Installation

System requirements

Minimum:

- Windows-based PC with CD drive and mouse

- Microsoft Windows® XP (32 bit), Windows®Vista (32 or 64 bit), or Windows® 7 operating system

- 512 MB RAM

- 510 MB (recommended full install) free hard disk space

- 1024 x 768 monitor resolution

Additional disk resources and memory are required when editing large or complex documents.

 To enjoy the full benefit of brushes and their textures, you'll need a computer whose processor supports SSE. On brush selection, an on-screen message will indicate if your computer is non-SSE.

Optional:

- Windows-compatible printer

- TWAIN-compatible scanner and/or digital camera

- Internet account and connection required for accessing online resources and scrapbook upload

Installation procedure

1. Insert the Program CD into your DVD/CD drive.

    - If AutoPlay is enabled on the drive, this automatically starts the Setup Wizard. Follow the on-screen instructions for install.

        -or-

    - If AutoPlay is not enabled (or doesn't start the install automatically), run **setup.exe** from your CD/DVD.

2. (Optional) If you've also purchased a **Digikit Collections DVD**, install it now by inserting it into your DVD drive.

Getting started

Using the Startup Wizard

Once you have installed Digital Scrapbook Artist, you're ready to start scrapbooking! By default, a **Serif Digital Scrapbook Artist** item is added to the **All Programs** submenu of the Windows **Start** menu.

Opening the Startup Wizard

- Use the Windows **Start** menu to open Digital Scrapbook Artist.

  - or -

- On the **File** menu, click **New>New from Startup Wizard...**

The Startup Wizard offers different routes into the program:

Option	Allows you to...
Start with a theme	Use a Digikit layout as the basis for your scrapbook. You can customize the layout to suit your needs by adding your own photos, text, and decorative items.
Open saved work	Open and edit your saved scrapbooks.
Start with a blank page	Open a new blank page in the workspace.
Online Tutorials	Go directly to the Getting Started tutorials.

Turning the Startup Wizard off and on

If you don't want the Startup Wizard to display every time you open Digital Scrapbook Artist, you can turn it off.

To turn off the Startup Wizard:

- In the lower-left corner of the Startup Wizard, click **Don't show this wizard again**.

- or -

1. On the **Tools** menu, click **Options...**

2. In the **Options** dialog, under **Ease of Use**, clear the **Startup Wizard** check box.

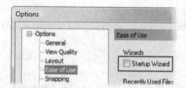

 Both methods only turn the Startup Wizard off when you open Digital Scrapbook Artist. Once the program is open, you can still access the Startup Wizard by clicking **File>New>New from Startup Wizard**.

To turn the Startup Wizard back on:

1. On the **Tools** menu, click **Options...**

2. In the **Options** dialog, under **Ease of Use**, select the **Startup Wizard** check box.

- or -

1. On the **File** menu, click **New>New from Startup Wizard**.

2. Click to clear the **Don't show this wizard again** box.

Starting from a Digikit theme

Digikits offer a selection of themed page layouts, backgrounds, frames, materials, letters, embellishments, brushes, swatches, and effects.

If you want to get started quickly, selecting a Digikit theme will help you to create your first scrapbook in just a few easy steps.

You can also create original scrapbooks from scratch. See *Starting a scrapbook from scratch* on p. 27.

 Additional Digikits are available from the **w**ww.daisytrail.com website.

Choosing your theme and layout

1. Launch Digital Scrapbook Artist, or click **File>New from Startup Wizard...**

2. In the Startup Wizard, click **Start with a Theme**.

3. In the **Digikit Browser** dialog, in the upper-left **Scrapbook Name** box, type a name for your scrapbook.

4. In the **Page Size** drop-down list, select a page size.

5. In the **Digikit Browser** dialog you'll see installed Digikits, plus featured free and purchasable Digikits from the DaisyTrail.com shop. (See *Buying Digikits* on p. 54.)

⊙ Select the Digikit you want to use as the basis for your scrapbook by clicking its thumbnail.

⊙ In the **Layouts** section, select the pages you want to add to your scrapbook by clicking their thumbnails.

⊙ When you're finished selecting pages, click **Done**.

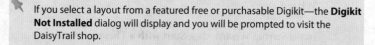

If you select a layout from a featured free or purchasable Digikit—the **Digikit Not Installed** dialog will display and you will be prompted to visit the DaisyTrail shop.

Once you've installed your free or purchased Digikit, it will appear in the **My Digikits** section of the Digikit Browser. (See *Buying Digikits* on p. 54.)

The first page of the layout opens in the workspace, and all of the scrapbooking items contained in the Digikit are added to the Content tabs at the left of the workspace.

6. Running horizontally along the lower edge of the workspace, the **Pages** tab displays the pages you chose to add to your scrapbook.

   Click through the thumbnails to view these pages in the workspace and choose the page you want to work on first.

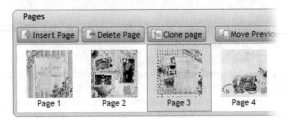

Before making any changes to the layout, let's save the file. (It's good practice to save your work frequently.)

Saving your work

The first time you save your work:

1. On the Standard toolbar, click **Save**.

2. In the **Save As** dialog:

    -   The **File name** text box displays the name you typed in the **Digikit Browser** dialog. To save your scrapbook with different file name, type it here.

    -   Browse to and select the destination for your saved file.

    -   Click **Save**.

 Digital Scrapbook Artist periodically autosaves your work to a temporary file, allowing you to recover as much as possible in the event of a system failure. You can set autosave frequency under the **General** option of the **Tools>Options...** dialog.

On subsequent saves:

-   To save the scrapbook under its current name, click the **Save** button. The existing scrapbook file is overwritten with your recent changes.

-   To save the scrapbook under a different name, click **File>Save As...** to open the **Save As** dialog.

 Scrapbooks are saved as files exclusively for use with Digital Scrapbook Artist, with a *.sbp file extension.

Adding your own photos

1. In the Content tabs at the left of the workspace, click the **Photos** tab to open it. At the bottom of the tab, click **Add.**

2. In the **Open** dialog, browse to and select the photos you want to add to your scrapbook.

   - To select multiple adjacent files, press and hold down the **Shift** key, click the first file in the list, and then click the last file.

   - To select multiple non-adjacent files, press and hold down the **Ctrl** key, and then click to select.

   - Click **Open**. Your photos are added to the **Photos** tab.

 To remove a photo from the **Photos** tab, click its **Remove** button.

Adjusting and replacing framed photos

1. Select the framed photo, and then click the **Crop** button.

2. To rotate, or zoom into or out of the photo, click the buttons displayed at the right edge of the photo.

3. To pan the photo, click and drag on it.

4. To close the Crop window, click ⬑ **Back**, or click elsewhere on the page or pasteboard area.

To replace a photo:

● Drag a different photo onto a frame from the **Photos** tab.

-or-

1. Select the framed photo you want to replace, and then click the 🖼️ **Select Cropped Object(s)** button that displays below it.

2. Click the 🖼️ **Replace Photo** button on the Photo context toolbar.

3. Browse to and select the photo you want to add and click **Open**.

Adding scrapbook letters

1. In the Content tabs at the left of the workspace, open the **Letters** tab.

2. To add an individual letter, drag it from the tab onto your page.

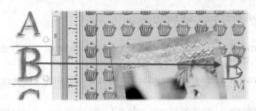

- or -

To add an entire word or phrase all at once, type your text into the box at the bottom of the tab, and then click **Insert**.

> To add a special character to your page, you will need to drag it directly from the **Letters** tab.

3. You can move, resize, rotate, and delete letters individually, or you can work with them as a group by first clicking the ⊞ **Group** button. (See *Grouping items* on p. 252.)

To work with grouped and ungrouped letters:

⊙ To **move** an individual letter or a group of letters, simply drag it.

⊙ To **resize** a letter or group, select it, and then drag a corner handle.

⊙ To **rotate** a letter or group, select it, and then drag its rotate handle.

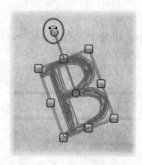

⊙ To **delete** a letter or group, select it and press the **Delete** key.

⊙ To **group** letters, click and drag to draw a selection marquee around them. (To avoid selecting the object beneath the letters, hold down the **Alt** key as you drag.)

Release the mouse button and then click the ⊞ **Group** button.

⊙ To **ungroup**, select the group and click the ⊞ **Ungroup** button.

To create your own letters, see *Creating your own Digikits* on p. 56.

Adding decorative items

1. In the Content tabs at the left of the workspace, open the **Embellishments** or the **Materials** tab.

2. Scroll the tab to find the item you want to add, and then drag it onto your page.

3. To move, resize, rotate, or delete an item, use the methods described above in Adding scrapbook letters.

 To remove a scrapbook item from a Content tab, click its **Remove** button.

 To create your own embellishments, see *Creating your own Digikits* on p. 56.

Adding drop shadows and effects

1. Select the item to which you want to add a drop shadow.

2. In the Studio tabs at the right of the workspace, click the **Effects** tab.

3. At the top of the tab, in the drop-down list, select the **Digikit** category. This category contains the preset effects included in your selected Digikit, and used in the default layouts.

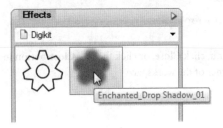

4. Click an effect thumbnail to apply it to your selected item.

Sharing your scrapbook

To share your scrapbook, you need to do the following:

1. Register on the www.daisytrail.com website.

2. Set up account information in Scrapbook Artist.

3. Upload your pages to the website.

For step-by-step instructions, see *Sharing via website* on p. 257.

Closing the program

To close the current scrapbook:

* On the **File** menu, click **Close**, or click the [×] **Close** button in the upper right corner of the workspace.

  - or -

  If you have a middle mouse button/wheel, and multiple scrapbooks open, hover over the document's tab and click the middle mouse button.

If the scrapbook is unsaved or has unsaved changes, you'll be prompted to save it.

To close Digital Scrapbook Artist:

- On the **File** menu, click **Exit**, or click the [X] **Close** button in the upper-right corner of the Digital Scrapbook Artist window.
For each open scrapbook, you'll be prompted to save any changes made since the last save.

Starting a scrapbook from scratch

If you create your scrapbook from scratch, the first step is to select your page background(s). Digital Scrapbook Artist Digikits provide a selection of backgrounds from which to choose.

Choosing page backgrounds

1. Launch Digital Scrapbook Artist, or click **File>New>New from Startup Wizard...**

2. In the Startup Wizard, click **Start with a blank page**.

   If you've switched the Startup Wizard off (and don't see it when you start up), you can switch it on again. Click **Tools>Options**, select the **Ease of Use** option, and then select the **Startup Wizard** check box.

3. In the **Digikit Browser,** you'll see installed Digikits, plus featured free and purchasable Digikits. (See *Buying Digikits* on p. 54.) Select the Digikit you want to browse by clicking its thumbnail.

4. Click the background(s) that you want to use in your scrapbook.

5. (Optional) To add all items from the Digikit, click ✔ **Add all items**.

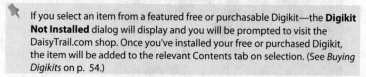

   If you select an item from a featured free or purchasable Digikit—the **Digikit Not Installed** dialog will display and you will be prompted to visit the DaisyTrail.com shop. Once you've installed your free or purchased Digikit, the item will be added to the relevant Contents tab on selection. (See *Buying Digikits* on p. 54.)

6. (Optional) Click ⊕ **Back to all Digikits** to add backgrounds from other Digikits.

7. When you've finished selecting backgrounds, click **Done**.

8. Drag the background you want to use onto the blank page displayed in the workspace.

   To change the background, simply drag a new one onto the page.

To remove a background from the **Backgrounds** tab, click its **Remove** button.

Before we go any further, let's save the file.

Saving your work

The first time you save your work:

1. On the Standard toolbar, click **Save**.

2. In the **Save As** dialog:

    - In the **File name** text box, type a file name or accept the default file name, e.g., Scrapbook1.

    - Browse to and select the destination for your saved file.

    - Click **Save**.

 Digital Scrapbook Artist periodically autosaves your work to a temporary file, allowing you to recover as much as possible in the event of a system failure. You can set autosave frequency under the **General** option of the **Tools>Options...** dialog.

On subsequent saves:

    - To save the scrapbook under its current name, click the **Save** button. The existing scrapbook file is overwritten with your recent changes.

    - To save the scrapbook under a different name, click **File>Save As...** to open the **Save As** dialog.

 Scrapbooks are saved as files exclusively for use with Digital Scrapbook Artist, with a *.sbp file extension.

Adding photo frames

1.   In the Content tabs at the left of the workspace, click the **Frames** tab to open it.

2.   On the **Frames** tab, click **Add...**

3.   The **Digikit Browser** opens to display frames, categorized by the name of the Digikit to which they belong. Scroll to the Digikit category you want to add frames from. You can add frames from more than one Digikit.

4.   Click a frame to add it to your scrapbook project, or click 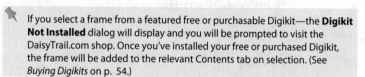 **Add all items** to add them all. The selected frames are added to the **Frames** tab.

> If you select a frame from a featured free or purchasable Digikit—the **Digikit Not Installed** dialog will display and you will be prompted to visit the DaisyTrail.com shop. Once you've installed your free or purchased Digikit, the frame will be added to the relevant Contents tab on selection. (See *Buying Digikits* on p. 54.)

5.   When you've finished selecting frames, click **Done**.

6.   Drag a frame from the **Frames** tab onto your page.

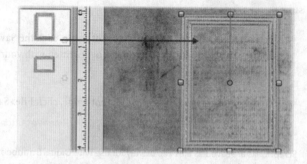

Once the frame is added to the page, you can move, resize, and rotate it. (See *Arranging items* on p. 245.)

To create your own photo frames, see *Creating your own photo frames* on p. 121.

 To remove a frame from the **Frames** tab, click its **Remove** button.

Adding photos

1. In the Content tabs at the left of the workspace, click the **Photos** tab to open it. At the bottom of the tab, click **Add...**

2. In the **Open** dialog, browse to and select the photos you want to add.

    - To select multiple adjacent files, press and hold down the **Shift** key, click the first file in the list, and then click the last file.

    - To select multiple non-adjacent files, press and hold down the **Ctrl** key, and then click to select.

3. Click **Open**. Your photos are added to the **Photos** tab.

 To remove a photo from the **Photos** tab, click its **Remove** button.

4. Drag a photo from the **Photos** tab and drop it onto the frame, or onto the page if you don't want to frame your photo.

5. (Optional) You can adjust your photo inside its frame, or even replace it if required. For details, see *Adjusting framed photos* on p. 118).

Adding decorative items

1. In the Content tabs at the left of the workspace, click the **Embellishments** or **Materials** tab to open it.

2. At the bottom of either tab, click **Add...**

3. The **Digikit Browser** opens to display **Embellishments** or **Materials**, categorized according to the Digikit to which they belong.

   Select the category from which you want to add items. (You can add items from more than one Digikit.)

4. Click an item to add it to your scrapbook project, or click 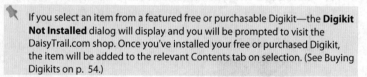 **Add all items** to add them all.

> If you select an item from a featured free or purchasable Digikit—the **Digikit Not Installed** dialog will display and you will be prompted to visit the DaisyTrail.com shop. Once you've installed your free or purchased Digikit, the item will be added to the relevant Contents tab on selection. (See Buying Digikits on p. 54.)

In the workspace, the items you added are displayed in the relevant Contents tab.

5. When you've finished selecting items, click **Done**.

6. To add an item to your page, drag it from its tab.

7. Once an item is placed on the page, you can move, resize, and rotate it as required. (See *Arranging items* on p. 245.)

> To create your own embellishments and materials, see Creating your own Digikits on p. 56.

> To remove a scrapbook item from a tab, click its ♻ **Remove** button.

Adding scrapbook letters

1. In the Content tabs at the left of the workspace, click the **Letters** tab to open it.

2. At the bottom of the **Letters** tab, click **Add...**

3. The **Digikit Browser** opens to display letters, which are categorized by the name of the Digikit to which they belong, e.g., Enchanted.

4. Scroll to the Digikit category you want to add letters from. You can add letters from more than one Digikit.

5. Click a letter to add it to your scrapbook project, or click ✔ **Add all items** to add them all. The selected letters are added to the **Letters** tab.

6. When you've finished selecting letters, click **Done**.

7. To add an individual letter, number or special character (such as an accent,) drag it from the tab directly onto your page.

    To add an entire word or phrase all at once, type your text into the box at the bottom of the tab, and then click **Insert**.

 To add a special character to your page, you will need to drag it directly from the tab.

 To remove a letter from the **Letters** tab, click its 🔄 **Remove** button.

 To create your own letters, see *Creating your own Digikits* on p. 56

You can now move, resize, rotate, and delete these letters individually, or you can work with them as a group by first clicking the  **Group** button. (See *Grouping items* on p. 252.)

Applying drop shadows and other effects

To add effects to your project:

1. On the **Pages** context toolbar, click **Add items from Digikits**. The **Digikit Browser** dialog opens.

2. Select the Digikit from which you want to add effects.

3. Scroll to the **Effects** category and click on an effect to add it to the **Digikit** category of the **Effects** tab.

4. (Optional) Click **Back to all Digikits** to add effects from other Digikits.

5. When you've finished selecting effects, click **Done**.

To apply an effect to a selected item:

1. Select the item to which you want to add a drop shadow or other effect.

2. In the Studio tabs at the right of the workspace, click the **Effects** tab.

3. At the top of the tab, in the drop-down list, select the **Digikit** category. You will see the effects you have added via the **Digikit Browser** dialog.

4. Click an effect thumbnail to apply it to your selected item.

original   drop shadow applied

Applying transparency

You can apply transparency quickly and easily using a slider on the **Color** tab. For more advanced effects, use the **Transparency Tool** (see online Help).

To apply transparency from the Color tab:

1. On the Standard toolbar, click the 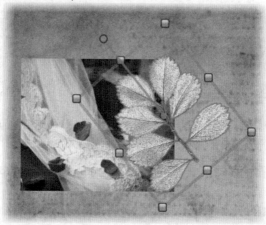 **Select** tool, and then click to select the item you want to work with.

2. On the **Color** tab, drag the Transparency slider to achieve the desired effect.

Adding text

1.   On the Standard toolbar, click the 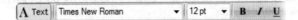 **Text** tool.

2.   To create text at the default size, click on your page to set a text insertion point.

     - or -

     Click and drag on your page to set the size of the text insertion point.

3.   To set text attributes (font, size, etc.) before typing: Make your selections on the Text context toolbar. (See *Formatting text* on p. 134.)

4.   To set text color, set the Line/Fill swatches on the **Color** tab. (See *Changing line and fill color* on p. 225.)

5.   Start typing.

> You can also create **Shape Text**, by typing directly inside a QuickShape or drawn shape. See *Adding text* on p. 127.

Creating brush strokes

1.   On the Standard toolbar, click the  **Brush** tool.

2.   At the right of the workspace, open the **Brushes** tab and select a brush category from the upper drop-down list.

3.   On the Brush context toolbar, set the brush stroke properties (width, opacity, smoothness, etc.).

4. Drag a brush stroke across your page.

5. To create a new brush stroke, repeat the click and drag process.

6. When you've finished painting, to deselect the brush stroke press the **Esc** key.

 Brushes used in the current scrapbook are added to the **Document** category of the **Brushes** tab.

For more on brushes, see *Adding brush strokes* on p.209.

Adding Digikit brushes

The **Brushes** tab's **Digikit** category displays the brushes added from Digikits. If you've previously chosen to add all the items from a Digikit, a selection of brush strokes will be displayed in this category.

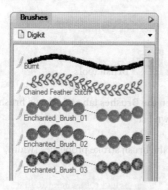

To add Digikit brushes:

1. On the **Pages Context** toolbar, click ![icon] **Add items from Digikits**. The **Digikit Browser** dialog opens.

2. Select a Digikit from which you want to add brushes, e.g., Enchanted.

3. Scroll to the **Brushes** category, and then click to select the brush(es) you want to use.

> If you select a brush from a featured free or purchasable Digikit—the **Digikit Not Installed** dialog will display and you will be prompted to visit the DaisyTrail.com shop. Once you've installed your free or purchased Digikit, the brush will be added to the **Digikit** category of the **Brushes** tab on selection. (See *Buying Digikits* on p. 54.)

4. (Optional) Click ![icon] **Back to all Digikits** to add brushes from other Digikits.

5. When you've finished selecting brushes, click **Done**.

Arranging items and groups on the page

●   To select a single item, click the ![icon] **Select** tool, and then click the item or group.

●   To select multiple items, click the ![icon] **Select** tool, click the first item, hold down the **Shift** key and click to select additional items.

- or -

Click in a blank area of the page, and then drag a selection marquee
around the items you want to select.

- To move an item or group, select it, and then drag it.

- To resize an item or group, select it and drag a corner resize
  handle.

- To rotate an item or group, select it, and then drag its rotate handle.

- To delete an item or group, select it, and then press the **Delete** key.

See also *Rotating and shearing items* (p. 247), *Ordering items* (p. 250), and *Grouping items* (p. 252).

Adding pages

1. On the **Pages** tab, select the page after which you want to add your new page.

2. Click  **Insert Page** to create a new blank page.

Pages

Insert Page   Delete Page

Page 1   Page 2

- or -

Click 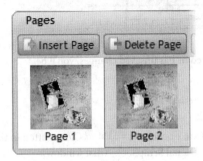 **Copy Page** to create a copy of the selected page.

Pages

Insert Page   Delete Page

Page 1   Page 2

See also *Adding and deleting pages* on p. 72.

Sharing your scrapbook

To share your scrapbook, you need to do the following:

1. Register on the www.daisytrail.com website.

2. Set up account information in Scrapbook Artist.

3. Upload your pages to the website.

For step-by-step instructions, see *Sharing via website* on p. 257.

Closing the program

To close the current scrapbook:

● On the **File** menu, click **Close**, or click the ⊠ **Close** button in the upper right corner of the workspace.

  - or -

If you have a middle mouse button/wheel, and multiple scrapbooks open, hover over the document's tab and click the middle mouse button.

If the scrapbook is unsaved or has unsaved changes, you'll be prompted to save it.

To close Digital Scrapbook Artist:

● On the **File** menu, click **Exit**, or click the ☒ **Close** button in the upper-right corner of the Digital Scrapbook Artist window.

For each open scrapbook, you'll be prompted to save any changes made since the last save.

Opening and displaying scrapbooks

You can open an existing scrapbook from the Startup Wizard or the File menu. If you have more than one scrapbook open, you can switch between them using the **Window** menu or the document tabs.

Opening a scrapbook from the Startup Wizard

1. Click the **Open Saved Work** option.

2. In the **Open Saved Work** dialog, in the left **Documents** pane:

    ⦿ Use the **Folders** tab to browse your computer's folder structure and locate your scrapbooks.

    - or -

    ⦿ Use the **History** tab to view your most recently used scrapbooks.

    On the right, preview thumbnails of your saved scrapbooks display.

    You can choose between **Thumbnails View** (displays thumbnails only), or **Details View** (displays thumbnails and information about the file—file size, creation date, and so on).

Click a thumbnail, and then click **Open**.

Opening a scrapbook from the File menu

1. On the **File** menu, click **Open...**

2. In the **Open** dialog, navigate to and select the scrapbook file you want to open, and then click **Open**.

Displaying scrapbooks

If you open multiple scrapbooks at the same time, there are several ways to jump between them quickly.

Displaying a scrapbook from the Window menu:

● Select a scrapbook name from the **Window** menu.

 Unsaved scrapbooks are indicated with an asterisk.

The currently active scrapbook is indicated with a check mark.

Displaying a scrapbook from the document tabs:

● In the upper left area of the workspace, click on an open scrapbook's tab to make it active. The file names of scrapbooks that are not active are grayed out.

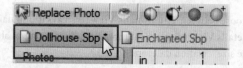

Digikits

Browsing

The **Digikit Browser** provides access to your installed Digikits, and to
featured free and purchasable Digikits from **daisytrail.com**. You can browse
Digikits and preview the items they contain, before adding them to your
workspace.

You can also use the search controls at the right of the dialog to narrow your
search, or to find a specific item. There are two ways to browse Digikit
items—by Digikit, or by item category.

Browsing Digikits

1.   On the Pages context toolbar, click **Add items from Digikits**.

2.   In the **Digikit Browser**, you'll see installed Digikits, plus featured free
     and purchasable Digikits from the DaisyTrail.com shop. (See *Buying
     Digikits* on p. 54.)

     Select the Digikit you want to browse by clicking its thumbnail.

3.   Scroll through the categories to browse items included in the Digikit.

4.   (Optional) To narrow your search, find items you have tagged, or to
     find a specific item—apply a search filter (see below).

5.   To browse another Digikit, click **Back to All Digikits**.

Browsing items

1.   In the lower-left corner of the **Digikit Browser** dialog, click **Add
     Digikit**.

2.   In the **Digikit Browser** dialog, click the **Browse my items** tab. You'll
     see items belonging to installed Digikits, plus featured free and

purchasable Digikits from the DaisyTrail.com shop. (See *Buying Digikits* on p. 54.)

3. On the left-hand side of the dialog, select an item category you want to browse, e.g., **Embellishments**.

4. The items are categorized further by the name of the Digikit to which they belong, e.g., Doll House. Scroll through to browse the items included in each Digikit. To make browsing easier, you can expand and collapse the Digikit categories to hide or reveal the items.

5. (Optional) To narrow your search, find items you have tagged, or to find a specific item—apply a search filter (see below).

Applying a search filter

The filter searches preset and custom tags applied to all of the Digikits shown in the **Digikit Browser** (this includes Digikits you have installed, and Digikits available from the DaisyTrail.com website). (See *Tagging Digikits* on p. 66.)

1. Click ⊕ **Add items from Digikits**.

2. Click **Browse Digikits** or **Browse my items**, depending on which browsing method you prefer.

3. There are two methods by which you can apply search filters, and both can be used together to further narrow your search.

   • Select a search tag from the drop-down menus.

   • Type the word or letter you want to search for in the **Search** text box, situated at the right of the dialog.

Search	🔍
cotton	✕

Ctrl-click to select more than one filter. Click  to remove the filter(s).

If you've searched via the **Browse Digikits** tab, the Digikit containing the relevant items is displayed for you to select and browse further.

◢ Featured Free DaisyTrail.com Digikits

Independence Day

◢ DaisyTrail.com Digikits

Cupid

If you've searched via the **Browse my items** tab, click on each category, e.g., **Frames**, to reveal the relevant items.

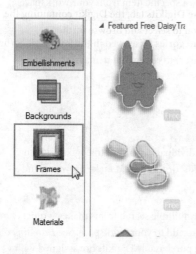

Adding items to your workspace

- To add items to your workspace via the **Browse Digikits** tab, select the Digikit you want to browse and then click the item you want to add.

- To add items to your workspace via the **Browse my items** tab, select the category you want to browse, and then click the item.

- Click ⊕ **Add Digikit** (displayed in the lower-left corner of the **Digikit Browser**) to add all items from a selected Digikit.

- Click ✓ **Add all items** (displayed in the upper-right corner of each category's thumbnail gallery) to add all items in the category.

> If you select an item, or add all items, from a featured free or purchasable Digikit—the **Digikit Not Installed** dialog will display and you will be prompted to visit the DaisyTrail.com shop. Once you've installed your free or purchased Digikit, the item will be added to the relevant Contents tab on selection. (See *Buying Digikits* on p. 54.)

- Click ♻ **Remove** (in the **Digikit Browser** or on the relevant Contents tab) to remove a specific item from your workspace..

- Click ⊖ **Clear All Categories** (displayed in the lower-left corner of the the **Digikit Browser**) to remove all items from your workspace.

Tagging

You can add searchable tags to individual items, and to Digikits, via the **Digikit Creator**. Tags are keywords, or terms, that make browsing and selecting items easier.

Grouping items or Digikits under multiple search terms makes it quicker and easier to find the items you want to add to your workspace. See *Browsing* on p. 47. Installed, featured free and purchasable Digikits are assigned with preset tags—but you can also add your own custom tags, as well as tagging your own custom items and Digikits. See *Creating your own Digikits* on p.56.

To tag an item

1. On the Pages context toolbar, click 🖉 **Digikit Creator**.

2. (Optional) If you're not already working with the Digikit you want to tag, click **Load Digikit** and load the relevant Digikit. See *Loading Digikits* on p. 67.

3. Select the item you want to tag by clicking its thumbnail.

4. In the text box at the bottom of the **Tags** pane, type search terms you want to apply to the item.

   You can apply as many tags as you need.

5. Click **Add**.

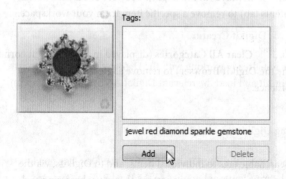

jewel red diamond sparkle gemstone

> To add more tags, simply repeat the previous two steps.

6. When you've finished tagging, save your Digikit. (See *Saving Digikits* on p. 66.)

The tags are now active and can be used as filters to search for your items in the **Digikit Browser**.

> To delete a tag, select it in the **Tags** pane and click **Delete**.

To tag a Digikit

1. Click 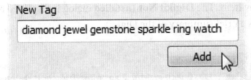 **Digikit Creator**.

2. If you're not already working with the Digikit you want to tag, click **Load Digikit** and load the relevant Digikit. See *Loading Digikits* on p. 67.

3. Click **Tag Digikit**.

4. At the bottom of the **Tag Digikit** dialog, in the **New Tag** text box, type in search terms you want applied to the Digikit. You can apply as many tags as you need.

5. Click **Add**.

New Tag

    diamond jewel gemstone sparkle ring watch

                                    Add

- To add more tags, simply repeat the previous two steps.

- To delete a tag, select it in the **Current Tags** pane and click **Delete**.

6. When you've finished tagging, save your Digikit. (See *Saving Digikits* on p. 66.)

    The tags are now active and can be used as filters to search for your Digikit in the **Digikit Browser**.

Buying Digikits

You can buy Digikits from the DaisyTrail.com shop. Provided that you have an internet connection, the **Digikit Browser** will automatically update to display the Digikits currently available for purchase from the website.

1. On the Pages context toolbar, click **Add items from Digikits**.

2. In the **Digikit Browser**, scroll to the **DaisyTrail.com Digikits** category.

3. Click the Digikit you want to buy and scroll through the categories to browse included items. You can also use the search controls on the right of the dialog to narrow the list of items, or search for a specific item. (See *Browsing* on p. 47.)

4. Click any item. The **Digikit Not Installed** dialog is displayed and provides a brief summary of the Digikit.

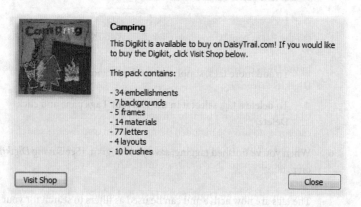

Camping

This Digikit is available to buy on DaisyTrail.com! If you would like to buy the Digikit, click Visit Shop below.

This pack contains:

- 34 embellishments
- 7 backgrounds
- 5 frames
- 14 materials
- 77 letters
- 4 layouts
- 10 brushes

Visit Shop   Close

5. Click **Visit Shop**. The DaisyTrail.com shop opens in your web browser for you to proceed with your purchase.

> If you've not already registered on DaisyTrail.com, you will have to **Register with DaisyTrail.**

If you don't want to immediately buy the Digikit, you can add the Digikit to a **Wishlist**—a list of items you want to have. You can return at a later date to make your purchase.

 Alternatively, rather than buying an individual kit, you can buy entire **Digikit Collections**.

Downloading free Digikits

Each month DaisyTrail.com offers a featured free Digikit or font for you to download to use in your projects.

Provided that you have an internet connection, the **Digikit Browser** will automatically update to display the Digikits currently available for free download. Digikits made available for free download are themed according to current or upcoming seasons, celebrations, public holidays, and vacations—Independence Day, Mother's Day, Father's Day, Easter, Christmas, Halloween, and so on.

To download a free Digikit:

1.   On the Pages context toolbar, click **Add items from Digikits**.

2.   In the **Digikit Browser**, scroll to the **Featured Free DaisyTrail.com Digikits** category.

3.   Click the Digikit you want to download and scroll through the categories to browse included items. You can also use the search controls on the right of the dialog to narrow the list of items, or search for a specific item. (See *Browsing* on p. 47.)

4.   Click any item. The **Digikit Not Installed** dialog is displayed and provides a brief summary of the Digikit.

5.   Click **Download**. DaisyTrail.com opens in your web browser for you to proceed with your free download.

If you've not already registered on DaisyTrail.com, you will have to **Register with DaisyTrail.**

Creating your own Digikits

Creating a Digikit

1. In **Digikit Browser**, browse your existing Digikits, and add the items you want to include in your custom Digikit to your workspace.

2. (Optional) In the main workspace, drag items you want to add to your Digikit from your page and drop them directly onto the appropriate Content tabs.

   For example, you may have previously added an item to your page as a photo, and now want to add it to the embellishments category of your new Digikit.

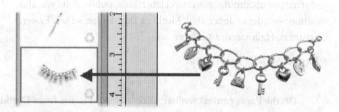

3. Click 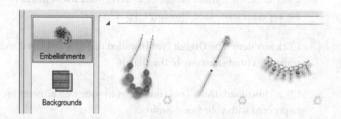 **Digikit Creator**.

   Items already added to the workspace display in the **Digikit Creator** window.

4. Choose a category from the list on the left, and then refer to the relevant section below to add your items

> You can create items from any of the supported image file formats, although one with good bit depth and transparency support (such as the PNG format) will produce the best results.

5. Tag your Digikit. See *Tagging Digikits* on p. 66.

6. Save your Digikit. See *Saving Digikits* on p. 66.

Adding embellishments & materials

1. In the category list on the left, click **Embellishments** or **Materials**.

   Items already added to your workspace display in the **Digikit Creator**.

2. Click **Import**.

3. To add individual files, click **Add Files**; to add all files contained in a folder, click **Add Folder**.

4. Browse to and select your file(s)/folder.

   - or -

   (**Embellishments** category only) Browse to and select a folder of assorted scrapbook items. Once you have added your items, you can sort them into their respective categories directly from the **Embellishments** pane (see step 6 below).

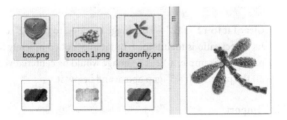

5. Click **Open/OK**.

The items are added to the **Digikit Creator** window. To rearrange items, click and drag them.

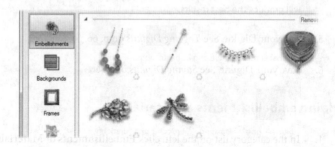

6. (Optional) If you added assorted items to the **Embellishments** category, drag the items into their respective categories on the left.

Adding backgrounds

1. In the category list on the left, click **Backgrounds**.

Backgrounds already added to your workspace display in the **Digikit Creator** window.

2. Decide how you want your background image to appear on the page:

- Select **Fit to 12" x 12"**—The image is **scaled to completely fill** a 12" x 12" page size. Its aspect ratio is maintained, but it may overlap the page edges (if not square).
  - or -

- Clear **Fit to 12" x 12"**—The image is **scaled to fit** a 12" x 12" page. Its aspect ratio is maintained, but it may not completely fill the page. For example, a 12" x 6" image would be centered vertically on the page, with a 3" gap above and below it.

3. Click **Import**.

4. To add individual files, click **Add Files**; to add all files contained in a folder, click **Add Folder**.

5. Browse to and select your file(s)/folder, and then click **Open/OK**.

The backgrounds are added to the **Digikit Creator** window. To rearrange backgrounds, click and drag them.

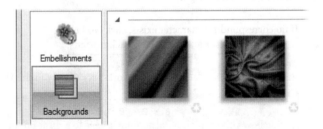

Adding frames

● See *Creating your own photo frames* on p. 121.

Adding and adjusting letters

You can add your own letters, numbers, and special characters to a Digikit—these may be imported as image files, or created on your page. You can also tweak the letters contained in any Digikit, whether you have created them or not.

Method 1: Importing letters

1. In **Digikit Creator**, in the category list on the left, click **Letters**.

   Letters already added to your workspace display in the **Digikit Creator** window.

2. Click **Import**.

3. To add individual files, click **Add Files**; to add all files contained in a folder, click **Add Folder**.

4. Browse to and select your file(s)/folder, and then click **Open/OK**.

5. In the **Keyboard** dialog, your letter displays on the left.

   Select the corresponding letter, number, or special character from the scrolling lists on the right.

   If no corresponding character exists, click **No Letter**.

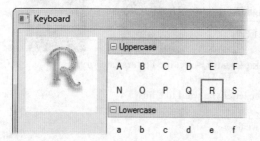

6. Click **OK**.

7. If you added multiple files, the next character displays. Repeat steps 5 and 6 until all characters are assigned.

8. Your letters are added to the **Digikit Creator** window. To rearrange your letters, click and drag them.

Method 2: Adding letters from your page

1. On your page, create your own letter, number, or special character.

2. Drag the letter onto the **Letters** tab.

3. Follow steps 5 to 7 described above.

4. Click **OK**.

5. Your letters are added to the **Letters** tab.

6. To save these letters to your Digikit, open **Digikit Creator** and save your Digikit. See *Saving Digikits* on p. 66.

Adjusting letters

1. In **Digikit Creator**, select the **Letters** category.

2. Select the letter you want to adjust.

3. Click **Tweak**.

4. In the **Tweak Letter** dialog, adjust baseline, assigned character, spacing, and offset values as required.

5. Click **OK**.

Adding layouts

Method 1: Adding from Digikit Creator

1. In **Digikit Creator**, in the category list on the left, click **Layouts**.

   Layouts already added to your workspace display in the **Digikit Creator** window.

2. Click **Add**.

3. The **Select Pages** dialog displays the layouts in the current scrapbook.

4. Select the pages you want to add as layouts and click **OK**.

   Your layouts are added to the **Digikit Creator** window.

Method 2: Adding from the main workspace

1. On the **Pages** tab at the bottom of the workspace, select the page you want to add as a layout.

   Click  **Add as a Digikit Layout**.

2. To save the new layout(s) to your Digikit, open **Digikit Creator** and save your Digikit. See *Saving Digikits* on p. 66.

Adding brushes

- See *Creating custom brushes* in online Help.

Adding swatches

You can add color swatches from the **Digikit Creator** (using the **Color Palette Designer**) or from the **Color** tab (using the **Color Picker** dialog).

Method 1: Adding swatches from Digikit Creator

1. In **Digikit Creator**, in the category list on the left, click **Swatches**.

   Swatches already added to your workspace display in the **Digikit Creator** window.

2. Click **Colors** to open the **Color Palette Designer**.

   On the right, the **Palette** gallery displays the swatches currently available in the Digikit palette.

3. To choose the base color for your new swatches, you can:

   - Click in the outer ring of the color wheel to choose a color hue, and then click inside the triangle to adjust the saturation and tint.

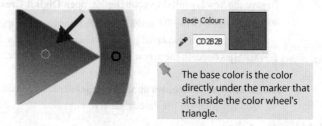

Base Colour:

CD2B2B

The base color is the color directly under the marker that sits inside the color wheel's triangle.

- Use the **Hue**, **Saturation**, and **Lightness**, or **Red**, **Green**, and **Blue** sliders or input boxes to adjust the **Base Color** swatch.

- Drag a color swatch from the displayed **Palette** gallery onto the **Base Color** swatch or onto the color wheel.

4. Select a color **Spread** from the drop-down list (for details on spread types, see *Using color palettes* on p. 238.)

5. **Optional:** Use the **Angle** and/or **Contrast** slider to modify the spread.

6. Once you're happy with the spread colors offered, you can use any of the following methods to add them to your palette:

- **Add all colors:** Click the **Add All** button to add all of the colors in the spread to the **Palette** gallery.

- **Individual color selection:** Click and drag individual colors from the spread directly onto the **Palette** gallery.

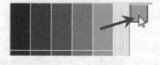

- **Add a range of colors:** Use the arrow selector control to select a range of colors from the spread.

Click either of the  small Rotate buttons to adjust the angle of the large arrow displayed on top of the grid. The range of colors that lies beneath the arrow will be added to the palette.

When you are happy with the range selected, click **Add Range** to add the colors to the **Palette** gallery.

7. When you have finished adding colors, click **OK** to close the **Color Palette Designer**.

The new swatches are added to the **Digikit Creator** window and displayed on the **Color** tab.

Method 2: Adding swatches from the Color tab

1. On the **Color** tab, right-click on the palette and click **Add...**

2. In the **Color Picker** dialog, you can use any of the following methods to mix your custom color:

   - Choose any color model from the **Models** drop-down list. Click and drag the vertical spectrum slider to set your base color, and then click in the large color box to define your new color.

   - Choose any color model from the **Models** drop-down list, and then type values into the **Components** boxes.

   - Select **RGB** from the **Models** drop-down list. Click the ✐ **Color Picker**, then hold down the mouse button and click anywhere in your workspace to pick up your new color.

The magnified color swatch updates as you drag. Release the mouse button to select the displayed color.

3. Click **OK**.

The new color is added to the **Color** tab palette.

4. To save the new palette swatch to your Digikit, open **Digikit Creator** and save your Digikit. See *Saving Digikits* on p. 66.

Tagging Digikits

● See *Tagging* on p. 66.

Saving Digikits

1. Use the procedures described above to add all your new items to the **Digikit Creator** dialog.

2. Click **Save Digikit**.

3. Name your new Digikit.

4. (Optional) By default, Digikits are saved to the **My Documents\My Digikits** folder. To save to a different location, click **Browse Folders**.

5. (Optional) By default, new Digikits are accessible from the **Digikit Browser**, but you can also make them available from the **Start with a theme** dialog.

- **Include in Start With a Theme dialog:** Select this check box if you want to include the Digikit in the **Start With a Theme** dialog.

 Your Digikit must include at least one layout for this option.

- **Exclude first layout from Digikit Browser:** Select this check box if you want to exclude the *first layout* (i.e., the cover page) from the **Digikit Browser**.

 Your Digikit must include at least two layouts for this option.

6. Click **Done**.
   You can now access your Digikit items from the **Digikit Browser**, and the **Start with a theme** dialog (if you selected this option in step 5).

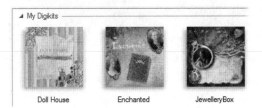

| Doll House | Enchanted | JewelleryBox |

Loading Digikits

From the **Digikit Creator** dialog, you can load any of your Digikits and add, adjust, and remove their items.

> ⚠ Note that any items currently added to your workspace, and to the **Digikit Creator** window, will be removed and replaced with the items from the loaded Digikit.

To load a Digikit:

1. In **Digikit Creator**, click **Load Digikit**.

2. Browse to locate the Digikit you want to work on and click **Open**.

Setting up and viewing your pages

4

Choosing page size

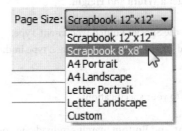

If you choose to use a scrapbook theme from the Startup Wizard (see p. 15), you can set your page size when you select your theme. Page size is set via a **Page Size** drop-down list in the **Digikit Browser** dialog.

Digital Scrapbook Artist offers all the popular scrapbooking page sizes. The **Scrapbook 8" x 8"** option gives you an 8" x 8" page size, which can be output to printers set up for US Letter or A4 page sizes without rescaling at time of print.

You can also create a non-standard page size by selecting the **Custom** option, and then setting your page size in the **Page Setup** dialog.

 You can change your page size at any time after you've created your scrapbook—but as a general rule, it's best to make page setup one of your first tasks.

You can change your page size at any time after you've created your scrapbook—but as a general rule, it's best to make page setup one of your first tasks.

If the Startup Wizard is turned off, or you cancel the wizard, a new blank scrapbook defaults to the 12" x 12" page size.

Changing page size via Page Setup

1. In the Startup Wizard, click **Start with a Theme**. In the **Digikit Browser** dialog, choose **Custom** from the **Page Size** drop-down list.

    -or-

    On the Pages context toolbar, click 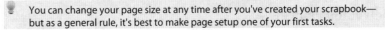 **Page Setup**.

2. Select a scrapbook category by enabling a **Document Type** option button. Choose from **Regular** or **Special Folded**.

- For **Regular** documents, select a **Document Size**, then set the orientation (**Portrait** or **Landscape**) if using a non-square page size. For a custom size, enter a **Width** and **Height**.

- For greetings cards, select the **Special Folded** Document Type, choose **Card** or **Tent Card**. You'll see previews of each type in the **Preview** window.

3. Adjust the scrapbook **Margins** to your specifications.

   You can set the **Left**, **Top**, **Right**, and **Bottom** margins individually, or click the **From Printer** button to derive the page margin settings from the current printer settings.

    Note: Page margins are represented on the page area by solid blue guides (top, bottom, left and right). To see them, you'll need to switch guides on via **Layout Guides** on the **View** menu.

4. Click **OK** to accept the new dimensions. The updated settings are applied to the current scrapbook.

Changing page units

The width, height, and margins of the scrapbook (its printing dimensions) are shown in **page units**—by default, inches. You can change the unit without altering the scrapbook's actual dimensions.

1. Click **Tools>Options...**

2. In the **Options** dialog, click **Layout**, and then make a selection from the **Ruler Units** drop-down list.

Adding, moving and deleting pages

A scrapbook can consist of a single page, or a series of pages made up of various layouts. You can add pages by adopting pre-designed layouts, or by adding your own blank pages. All pages are displayed in the Pages tab, which can be expanded from the bottom of your workspace.

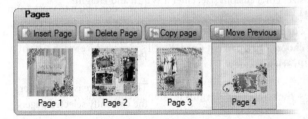

Adding new pre-designed layouts

Digital Scrapbook Artist offers a range of pre-designed Digikit layouts on which to base your scrapbook. You can also introduce layouts into your scrapbook as new pages. By customizing each new layout page, you can quickly create a professional looking scrapbook. See *Starting from a Digikit layout* on p. 17 for more information.

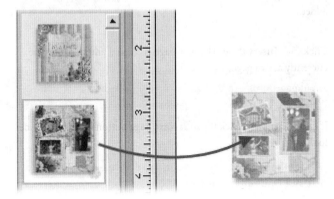

Adding blank pages

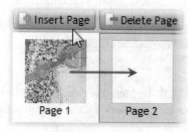

Page 1   Page 2

If you don't plan to work from a pre-designed layout, you can add blank pages from the Pages tab.

The new page is added after the currently selected page.

To expand the Pages tab:

• Click on the ▼ button at the bottom of the workspace. Click the button again to collapse the tab.

To add a new page:

1. On the **Pages** tab, select the page after which your new page will be added.

2. Click **Insert Page**. The new page is created and becomes the currently active page.

   -or-

   If on the last page, click the ▶ **Next Page** button on the HintLine toolbar.

Moving pages

Page 2   Page 3   Page 4

From the **Pages** tab, you can either:

- Click and drag a page to its new position in the tab (illustrated above).

  -or-

- Select a page selected and click 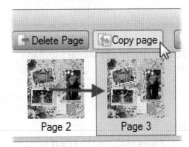 **Move Previous** or **Move Next**. The selected page jumps one position back or forward in the page order.

Deleting a selected page

On the **Pages** tab, select a page and click **Delete Page**, or right-click on the page and click **Delete**.

Copying pages

Use the **Copy page** button to base your new page on an existing page. Page items are copied across to the new page.

1. On the **Pages** tab, select the page you want to copy.

2. Click **Copy Page** to create an identical copy immediately after the selected page.

💡 You can reorder the pages by dragging and dropping them.

Panning and zooming

Use panning to move around zoomed-in areas of your scrapbook. To zoom, a variety of tools and magnifying options are available.

💡 If you use zooming and panning a lot, try using the Navigator tab, which is purposely designed for navigating around your scrapbook page.

Panning

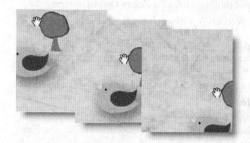

Click the **Pan Tool** on the HintLine toolbar, then use the hand cursor to click and drag anywhere on the page to reposition it in the window.

💡 If you're using a wheel mouse, you can hold down the middle button and drag anywhere on the page to reposition it in the window.

Zooming

Zoom tools on the **HintLine** toolbar allow you to view and/or edit the page at different levels of detail.

You can zoom in/out in increments, or by a user-defined or preset amount.

44% The **Current Zoom** setting on the HintLine toolbar displays the current zoom percentage, with 100% representing an actual-size page.

Click on the **Current Zoom** value to select a preset zoom from a pop-up menu (including fit to **Full Page** or **Page Width**), or type over the value for a custom zoom percentage.

To zoom to a particular view:

- On the HintLine toolbar, click ▇ **Zoom Out** to decrease the current zoom percentage with each click.

- Click ▇ **Zoom In** to increase the current zoom percentage with each click.

- Click the ▇ **Zoom Tool** and drag out a rectangular selection marquee on the page to define a region to zoom in to. The zoom percentage adjusts accordingly, fitting the designated region into the window.

  To zoom out, hold down the **Shift** key when dragging or just right-click on the page. You can also pan around a zoomed-in page while the **Ctrl** key is pressed. To zoom to the current selection, choose **Selection** from the **View** menu.

- Click the ▇ **Fit Page** button to adjust the zoom percentage so the entire page area is displayed in the window.

If you're using a wheel mouse, you can scroll the wheel forward or back to move up or down the page, or move horizontally left or right by using the **Shift** key and scrolling together. Try combining the **Ctrl** key and scrolling up or down for immediate in/out zoom control.

Navigating pages

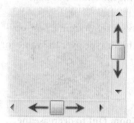

You can use the horizontal and vertical scroll bars to scroll the page and pasteboard area.

The Pages tab and HintLine toolbar provide additional controls to let you navigate between pages.

Navigating with the Pages tab

Once you have added pages, use the Pages tab to quickly navigate between pages.

1. To expand the **Pages** tab, click on the ▬▬▬▬ ▼ button at the bottom of the workspace.

    (Click the button again to collapse the tab.)

2. To view a specific page simply select its thumbnail.

Page 3

You can also use the page controls on the HintLine toolbar to navigate your pages. For details, see online Help.

Using design aids

Digital Scrapbook Artist provides a number of tools to assist you as you design your scrapbook. Typically the tools can be switched on or off as you design.

Rotating your canvas

Rotating your canvas helps you to maintain natural flow when drawing freeform lines, curves, or brush strokes, where the artist uses the wrist as a pivot (especially when using a pen tablet). If you rotate the canvas by a chosen angle then the drawing becomes easier—taking advantage of the natural arc of the drawing hand.

The above example illustrates how grass-like brush strokes can be added to a canvas once it has been rotated 25°!

To rotate your canvas:

Either:

1. Click the  **Rotate Canvas** button on the HintLine toolbar (don't click the down arrow).

2. Hover over your workspace until you see the cursor, then click and drag to rotate the canvas clockwise or counter-clockwise.

3. Once you're happy with the degree of rotation, release the mouse button to reposition the canvas.

    -or-

*   Click the down arrow on the ⬛ ▼ **Rotate Canvas** button (HintLine toolbar) and choose a preset angle from the drop-down list.

You can also select an item and then choose **To Item** from the **Rotate Canvas** drop-down list. The canvas adjusts so that the item is positioned square to the X and Y axes.

To reset your canvas:

*   With the button enabled, double-click on the canvas to reset.

Applying the Rule of Thirds

Traditionally a technique used in photography, the **Rule of Thirds** grid can also be applied to your scrapbook to help you with page composition.

By aligning items to intersecting horizontal and vertical lines (rather than just centering items on the page) you can create scrapbooks with greater visual interest.

When a grid is applied to your page the displayed context toolbar lets you alter the grid's color and opacity. You can also add more grids, delete, and reset a grid. (See online Help.)

 The grid is actually an overlay which appears as an 'Overlay Layer' in the Layers tab.

To apply a Rule of Thirds grid:

1. Click **Rule of Thirds** on the HintLine toolbar. A blue grid is overlaid over your page.

2. (Optional) Drag a corner or edge handle to resize the grid; reposition the grid by dragging. Use over selected items (instead of the entire page) depending on what you're currently working on.

3. Place embellishments, photos, or cut materials onto any of the intersecting blue lines.

If at any point the **Rule of Thirds** grid becomes deselected, simply click the **Rule of Thirds** button again to reselect it.

Isolating items

For focused editing, Digital Scrapbook Artist provides **Solo mode**. This allows you to temporarily isolate selected item(s) such as embellishments, or photo from the page and place them on a neutral background.

- Select the item(s), then click **Solo Mode** button on the **HintLine** toolbar. After editing, click the button again to return to normal editing mode.

Clipping items

Clipped mode cuts off (clips) items that hang over the edge of your canvas, and which would otherwise display on your gray pasteboard area. The option is turned on by default, but you can view your overlapping items unclipped if required.

To turn off Clipped mode:

- Disable the **Clipped Mode** button on the **HintLine** toolbar. Existing and new overlapping items will then display in full. Click the button again to return to **Clipped** mode.

Working with photos

5

Adding and positioning your photos

You can use the following methods to add photos to your project:

- Use the **Photos** tab to store photos that you want to use in your scrapbook. You can then drag them onto the page as you need them, or use AutoFlow (p. 114) to quickly add them to frames you have already placed on your page.

- Use the ▬▬ **Photo** button on the Standard toolbar to add individual images directly to the page.

> 💡 Use the first method if you want to add multiple photos to your project all at once, or if you want to add your photos to photo frames.
>
> Use the second method if you want to add photos to your page individually, or if you want to add your own embellishments to your layout.

Adding photos to the Photos tab

1. In the Contents tabs at the left of the workspace, click the **Photos** tab to open it. At the bottom of the tab, click **Add...**

2. In the **Open** dialog, browse to and select the photos you want to add to your scrapbook.

- To select multiple adjacent files, press and hold down the **Shift** key, click the first file in the list, and then click the last file.

- To select multiple non-adjacent files, press and hold down the **Ctrl** key, and then click to select.

3. Click **Open**. Your photos are added to the **Photos** tab.

Adding photos to the page

To add a photo from the Photos tab:

There are several ways to add photos to your page:

- Drag a photo from the **Photos** tab directly onto the page, or onto a photo frame. (See *Adding photo frames* on p. 109.)

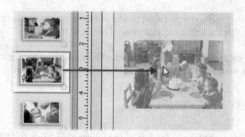

- Click **AutoFlow** to sequentially populate a series of photo frames with photos from the **Photos** tab. (See *Using AutoFlow* on p. 114.)

● Replace the contents of a photo frame by dragging a new photo onto the frame.

On the **Photos** tab, framed and unframed photos added to your scrapbook are denoted with a check mark icon.

To add a photo from the Standard toolbar:

1. On the Standard toolbar, click **Photo**.

   - or -

   On the **Insert** menu, click **Photo>From File...**

 You can also insert photos directly from an external device such as a camera or scanner. See *Importing camera and scanner images* in online Help.

2. In the **Open** dialog, browse to and select the photo you want to add, and then click **Open**.

3. To insert the photo at default size, simply click the mouse.

   - or -

   To set the photo size, drag out a region and release the mouse button.

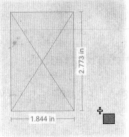

On the **Photos** tab, photos added to your scrapbook are denoted with a check mark icon.

Moving photos

1. Select the photo(s) with the  **Select** tool.

2. Click inside the photo (not on a handle), hold down the left mouse button, and then drag to a new location.

    (Note that the cursor changes to a ⌖ Move cursor.)

    - or -

    Click and drag the photo's ✥ **Move** button.

Replacing, resizing, and deleting photos

Once you've placed a photo on your page, you can replace, resize, or delete it as required.

Replacing photos

1. On the Standard toolbar, click the  **Select** tool, and then click to select the photo you want to replace.

2. On the Photo context toolbar, click **Replace Photo**.

3. In the **Open** dialog, browse to and select the photo you want to add, and then click **Open**.

To replace a framed photo:

- Drag a different photo onto the frame from the **Photos** tab, or use **AutoFlow** to automatically replace the contents of multiple frames in a single step. (See *Fitting photos to frames* on p. 113.)

Resizing photos

1. Select the photo with the  **Select** tool.

2. To resize the photo, drag a corner handle.

The photo's aspect ratio is preserved. To allow free resizing to any aspect ratio, hold down the **Shift** key while dragging.

Deleting photos

- To remove a photo from the page, select the photo and press the **Delete** key.

- To remove a photo from the Photos tab, click its 🔄 **Recycle** button.

For information on deleting framed photos, see *Deleting frames and framed photos* on p. 120.

Cropping your photos

Digital Scrapbook Artist includes the **Crop Tool** for cropping objects and photos on the page. The Crop context toolbar also provides a Rule of Thirds grid to help you with your photo composition.

 For information on working with framed photos, see *Fitting photos to frames* on p. 113.

Cropping a photo

1. Select a photo and then on the Standard toolbar, click the ⬚ **Crop Tool**.

2. Click and drag an edge or corner handle towards the center of the photo.

Using the Rule of Thirds

1. Select your photo and click the ⬚ **Crop Tool**.

2. On the Crop context toolbar, click ⊞ **Show/Hide Thirds Grid**.

3.   A 3 x 3 grid is superimposed on top of the photo.

4.   Drag an edge handle to crop the photo. As you do so, the grid repositions itself.

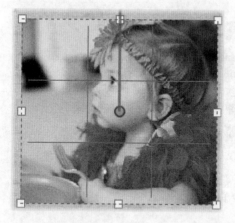

5.   Click and drag on the cropped photo to pan the image.

To zoom into or out of the image, use the Zoom tools displayed to the right of the photo.

For best results, aim to position your main subject of interest at a point where any two gridlines intersect.

Retouching photos

When you select a photo on the page, the Photo context toolbar displays.

In addition to replacing photos, this toolbar lets you quickly remove red eye, adjust brightness and contrast, apply auto level and auto contrast adjustments, and access PhotoLab (p. 94) and Cutout Studio (p. 102). You can use these tools on unframed and framed photos.

You can also convert unframed photos to "frameless" frames. (See *Converting photos to frames* on p. 120.)

For details, see online Help.

Applying PhotoLab filters

PhotoLab is a dedicated studio environment that lets you apply adjustment and effect filters to photos, individually or in combination.

PhotoLab offers the following key features:

- **Adjustment filters**
  Apply tonal, color, lens, and sharpening filters.

- **Effect filters**
  Apply distortion, blur, stylistic, noise, render, artistic, and various other effects.

- **Retouching filters**
  Apply red-eye and spot repair correction.

- **Non-destructive operation**
  All filters are applied without affecting the original photo, and can be edited at any point in the future.

- **Powerful filter combinations**
  Create combinations of mixed adjustment, retouching, and effect filters for savable workflows.

- **Selective masking**
  Apply filters to selected regions using masks.

- **Save and manage favorites**
  Save filter combinations to a handy **Favorites** tab.

- **Viewing controls**
  Compare before-and-after previews, with dual- and split-screen controls. Use pan and zoom control for moving around your photo.

- **Locking controls**
  Protect your applied filters from accidental change, then optionally apply them to other images on selection.

PhotoLab includes filter tabs, a main toolbar, and an applied filter stack around a central workspace.

Photos present in your scrapbook display in the **Images** tab, which is hidden by default. To display this tab, as illustrated below, simply click the ▬▬▼▬▬ button at the bottom of the dialog.

filter tabs   main toolbar   main workspace   filter stack

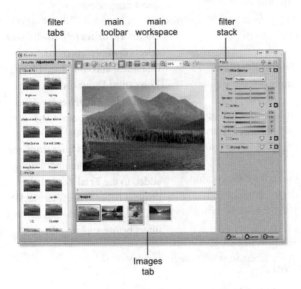

Images tab

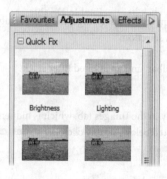

Filters are stored in the **Favorites**, **Adjustments**, and **Effects** filter tabs, and are grouped into categories.

For example, the **Adjustments** tab provides the **Quick Fix** and **Pro Edit** categories, while the **Effects** tab offers a wide range of creative effect categories.

On the **Favorites** tab, you'll find a selection of presets created with individual and combined filters. You can add your own custom filters to the **Favorites** tab. (See *Saving Favorites* on p. 101.)

When you apply a filter from one of these tabs, it is temporarily added to the **Trial Zone** that displays beneath the filter stack. This lets you preview and adjust filters before applying them.

Applying filters

1. Select the photo you want to work on. (If the photo is framed, select it and click 🖼 **Select Cropped Object**.)

2. Click 🔘 **PhotoLab** on the Photo context toolbar.

3. For ease of use, when you open PhotoLab, the **Filters** stack on the right contains some commonly-used filters (such as **White Balance** and **Lighting**). These filters are disabled by default.

To apply one of the default filters, click its  **Enable/Disable** control to enable it, and then adjust the filter settings by dragging the sliders.

To disable, reset, and delete a filter, see below.

To add a new filter:

1. Browse the filter thumbnails displayed on the **Favorites**, **Adjustments**, and **Effects** tabs, and click the one you want to apply.

   The selected filter is added to the **Trial Zone**, and the main window shows a preview of your photo with the filter applied.

2. Experiment with the filter settings in the **Trial Zone**—you can drag the sliders, or enter values directly—to suit your requirements. (Note that some filters also offer check boxes, drop-down menus, and additional advanced controls.)

3. (Optional) To replace the trial filter, click a different thumbnail.

   Selecting a new filter always replaces the current filter.

4. To apply the filter, click  **Commit** to add it to the **Filters** stack.

5. (Optional):

   - Repeat steps 1 to 4 to add more filters to the **Filters** stack.

     Filters are applied to a photo cumulatively, in the order in which they are added to the **Filter**s stack.

The most recently added filter always appears at the bottom of the stack. (See *To reorder filters*, below.)

- Disable, reset, and/or delete filters in the **Filters** stack. (See below.)

- Use zoom in/out buttons or a percentage magnification for detailed work.

- Use the retouch tools to fix red eye, remove blemishes, crop, and straighten. (See Retouching, below.)

6. To apply all filters in the **Filters** stack and close PhotoLab, click
   OK.

To disable, reset, and delete filters:

- To disable a filter, click ■ . Click □ to re-enable.

- To reset filter values, click ⮌ . Changes to settings revert to the filter's defaults.

- To delete a filter, click ✖ .

To reorder filters:

- Drag and drop your filter into any position in the stack. A dotted line indicates the new position in which the entry will be placed on mouse release.

To add a filter directly (without trialing):

- Click ⊕ **Add Quick Filter** at the top of the **Filters** stack and choose a filter from the flyout categories. The filter is applied directly to the stack without being added to the **Trial Zone**.

Retouching

PhotoLab's main toolbar provides some useful retouching tools. These are commonly used to correct photos before applying color correction and effects.

- **Red-eye tool**, to remove red eye from a human subject.

- **Spot-repair tool**, to remove blemishes from human skin and material surfaces.

For instructions on using the retouching tools, see online Help.

Selective masking

You may sometimes want to apply a filter to selected regions of a photo, rather than to the entire photo. In PhotoLab, you can do this by using a "mask" to define these region(s).

You can apply a mask:

- To the areas to which you want to apply the filter.

- or -

- To the areas you want to protect from the filter.

    In the following illustration, a mask has been used to protect the subject of the photo from a **Stained Glass** filter effect.

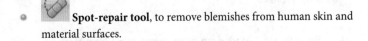

To apply a mask:

1. From the **Mask** drop-down menu, select **New Mask**.

2. In the **Tool Settings** pane, select the **Add Region** tool.

3. Adjust the settings to suit your requirements. For example, adjust **Brush Size** to paint larger or more intricate regions.

4. In the **Mode** drop-down menu, choose one of the following options:

   - **Select:** Choose this if you want to apply the filter only to the regions you paint. This is the default setting.

   - **Protect:** Choose this if you want to apply the filter to all areas of the photo, *except* for those that you paint.

5. Using the circular cursor, paint the regions to be masked (selected areas are painted in green; protected areas in red).

    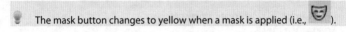

    If you've not been as accurate as you'd like while painting, click **Remove Regions** then paint over the unwanted painted regions.

6. Click ✔ to save your mask changes, or ✖ to cancel.

    💡 The mask button changes to yellow when a mask is applied (i.e.,).

You can create additional masks for the same filter, as above, and then choose between them. You can only apply one mask at any one time. By using the Mask menu's **New From>** option you can also base your new mask on an existing mask, which may be applied to the current filter or to any other filter in the stack. This is useful when working with **Favorites** filters that contain multiple adjustments.

To edit a mask:

● Expand the drop-down 🎭 **Mask** menu and select the mask you want to edit. Click **Edit Mask**.

Saving favorites

You can save specific filter settings, or combinations, as favorites for future use. PhotoLab stores all your favorites together in the **Favorites** tab. You can even create your own categories (e.g., My Adjustments) within the tab.

To save and manage favorites:

1. Click **Save Filter**.

2. In the dialog, type a name for your filter and choose the category in which to save it.

    (Click ⸬⸬⸬ to create a new category.)

3. (Optional) To organize your favorites into user-defined categories, click the ▷ **Tab Menu** button and choose **Manage Favorites**.

Using Cutout Studio

Digital Scrapbook Artist includes **Cutout Studio**, a powerful integrated solution for separating objects from their backgrounds.

Whether you're discarding or replacing a photo background, or isolating a section of an image to use in your layout, Cutout Studio lets you create eye-catching pictures quickly and easily.

> 🔖 You can also cut out your own photo frames using the **Frame Editor**, see *Creating your own photo frames* on p. 121.

Opening Cutout Studio

1. Select the photo you want to work with.

2. On the Photo context toolbar, click **Cutout Studio**.

3. Follow the instructions outlined below.

> 🔋 You'll find detailed instructions in the **Help** tab at the right of the Cutout Studio window.

Choosing your approach

The approach you take depends on your photo content.

 Discard Brush Tool

- If your subject of interest is placed against a simple, uniform background (sky, a wall, etc.), it's easier and quicker to **select and discard** the background.

 Keep Brush Tool

- If the subject of interest is surrounded by a background consisting of complex colors or patterns (such as trees or buildings), it's easier to **select and keep the subject.**

Selecting areas to discard or keep

To select areas to discard or keep:

1. Click the **Discard Tool** or the **Keep Tool**.

2. On the horizontal toolbar, select a brush size.

3.   (Optional) To adjust the degree of precision with which areas are selected, select the **Grow Tolerance** check box and adjust the value.

4.   Click and drag on the image to mark the areas you want to discard/keep. As you do so, Digital Scrapbook Artist locates similar adjoining areas and includes them in your selection.

5.   Repeat the click and drag process until your selection area is complete.

6.   As you paint your image, you can view your progress using the buttons on the left toolbar.

o   **Show original:** The default view mode. The image is shown in its original form.

o   **Show tinted:** Areas marked to be kept are shown with a green tint; areas to be discarded are shown with a red tint.

o   **Show transparent:** Areas marked for discarding are not shown. By default, these areas are replaced with a checkerboard background indicating transparency.

Choosing an output type

On the **Output Settings** tab, the **Output Type** drop-down list provides two output format options, **Alpha-edged bitmap**, and **Vector-cropped bitmap**. The format you choose depends on what you want to do with your resulting image.

General recommendations

Choose alpha-edged bitmap if you want to blend your cutout image into another image or background, or if your subject has poorly defined edges. Choose vector-cropped bitmap if you want to place your cutout image onto a plain or transparent background, or if your subject has more well-defined edges. (For more details on these output formats see online Help.)

To create an alpha-edged bitmap:

1. On the **Output Settings** tab, in the **Output Type** drop-down list, select **Alpha-edged Bitmap**.

2. (Optional)

   ◦ Drag the **Width** slider to set the area of the image that is to be faded into the background. (Use a lower **Width** setting for small images, or those with intricate edges; use a higher setting for large images, or those with 'cleaner' edges.)

   ◦ Drag the **Blur** slider to smooth out the cutout edge.

3. To preview the cutout area, click **Preview**.

4. (Optional) Use the touch-up tools to further refine the cutout area (alpha-edged bitmaps only). (See *Refining the cutout area* on p. 106.)

5. To complete the cutout and return to the Digital Scrapbook Artist workspace, click **OK**.

To create a vector-cropped bitmap:

1. On the **Output Settings** tab, in the **Output Type** drop-down list, select **Vector-cropped Bitmap**.

2. (Optional)

   ◦ Drag the **Feather** slider to adjust the softening effect around the edge of the cutout. This can improve the appearance of your image.

   ◦ Drag the **Smoothness** slider to smooth out the cutout edge.

   ◦ Drag the **Inflate** slider to adjust the cutout outline, moving it inward or outward.

> The **Inflate** adjustment is particularly useful if the edges of the subject include hair or fur, which usually also incorporate some of the background color.

3. To preview the cutout area, click **Preview**.

4. To complete the cutout and return to the Digital Scrapbook Artist workspace, click **OK**.

Refining the cutout area (alpha-edged bitmaps only)

1. On the **Output Setting** tab, click the **Preview** button. (You can use this button to check your cutout as you work.)

2. On the left toolbar, click the **Restore Touch-up Tool** or **Erase Touch-up Tool**.

3. Paint the areas for restoring or erasing as you would with the brush tools.

4. (Optional) To increase or decrease the opacity of the restored or erased areas, drag the **Hardness** slider (located on the horizontal toolbar).

   - Higher values will result in more pixels being erased, producing a more defined edge.

   - Lower values will produce a softer, more blended edge.

5. To complete the cutout and return to the Digital Scrapbook Artist workspace, click **OK**.

Editing the cutout area

If you've missed a portion of the photo intended to be discarded (or just removed too much), you can redefine the cutout area at any time.

To edit a cutout:

1. Select your photo and on the Photo context toolbar, click **Cutout Studio**. The existing cutout area is displayed.

2. Fine-tune your selection as described above.

Adding photos to frames

6

Adding photo frames to your scrapbook

Digital Scrapbook Artist Digikits include a wide selection of photo frames that you can add to your page. Once you've placed a frame on your page, simply drag a photo onto it—Digital Scrapbook Artist automatically fits the photo to the frame. All frames can be moved, resized, and rotated on the page.

Adding frames to the Frames tab

1. In the Content tabs at the left of the workspace, click the **Frames** tab to open it.

2. At the bottom of the **Frames** tab, click **Add...**

3. The **Digikit Browser** opens to display available frames, categorized by Digikit. Scroll to the Digikit from which you want to add frames. You can add frames from more than one Digikit.

4. Click a frame to add it to your scrapbook project, or click **Add all items** to add them all.

   The selected frames are added to the **Frames** tab.

5. Click **Done** to close the **Digikit Browser**.

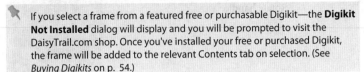

If you select a frame from a featured free or purchasable Digikit—the **Digikit Not Installed** dialog will display and you will be prompted to visit the DaisyTrail.com shop. Once you've installed your free or purchased Digikit, the frame will be added to the relevant Contents tab on selection. (See *Buying Digikits* on p. 54.)

Once the frame is added to the page, you can move, resize, and rotate it. (See *Arranging items* on p. 245.)

To create your own photo frames, see *Creating your own photo frames* on p. 121.

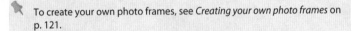

To remove a frame from the **Frames** tab, click its **Remove** button.

Adding frames to the page

1. Drag a frame from the **Frames** tab onto your page.

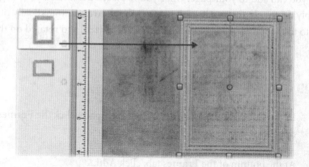

2. Once the frame is added to the page, there are various ways to work with it.

   ● To resize the frame, drag a corner handle.

   ● To rotate the frame, drag the Rotate handle.

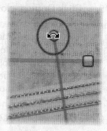

3. To add a photo to a frame, drag it from the **Photos** tab and drop it onto a frame.

    - or -

    Click **AutoFlow** to sequentially populate a series of photo frames with photos from the **Photos** tab. (See p. 114.)

Fitting photos to frames

Once you have added your photos to the **Photos** tab, you can frame them on the page—manually by clicking and dragging, or automatically using **AutoFlow**. Digital Scrapbook Artist lets you rotate, zoom, and pan your framed photos inside their frames. You can even crop a framed photo and adjust its frame to follow suit!

You can also convert photos so that they sit inside "frameless" frames. Once converted, these frames function exactly like the decorative frames you've added from the **Frames** tab. (See *Converting photos to frames* on p. 120.)

Adding individual photos to frames

1. Add your photo(s) to the **Photos** tab. (See *Adding photos to the Photos tab* on p. 85.)

2. Add a frame to your page. (See *Adding frames to your scrapbook* on p. 111.)

3. Drag a photo from the **Photos** tab and drop it onto the frame. Digital Scrapbook Artist fits the photo to the frame automatically.

On the **Photos** tab, photos added to your scrapbook are denoted with a check mark icon.

Using AutoFlow

1. Add your photo(s) to the **Photos** tab. (See *Adding photos to the Photos tab* on p. 85.)

2. Add a frame to your page. (See *Adding frames to your scrapbook* on p. 111.)

3. On the **Photos** tab, click **AutoFlow** to automatically populate multiple photo frames.

4. The **AutoFlow Photos Into Frames** dialog opens, offering various options for filling your frames. For example, you can choose to replace existing photos in frames; randomize photo order; insert new pages to accommodate extra photos, and so on.

   Select any options you want to apply and click **OK**.

   - Frames are filled sequentially, from back to front in the **Z-order** (see *Ordering items* on p. 250).

     This means that if you haven't rearranged your frames (using the **Arrange** tab or the **Arrange>Order Items...** menu), they will be filled in the order in which you added them to your page.

   - By default, photos are placed in available frames in the order they appear on the **Photos** tab (unless you selected the **Randomize photo order** fill option).

5. If you have more frames than photos, or vice versa, a dialog will display.

   - If you have more frames than photos: Delete the unused frames, or add more photos and then drag them from the **Photos** tab and drop them onto the frames.

   - If you have more photos than frames: Add more frames to your page, and then drag the photos from the **Photos** tab and drop them onto the frames.

On the **Photos** tab, photos added to your scrapbook are denoted with a check mark icon.

Cropping framed photos

1. Select the framed photo with the **Select** tool.

2.   Click  **Crop**.

3.   Drag the handles to crop the photo.

(See also *Cropping photos* on p. 171.)

4.   Click **Back** to return to the **Select** tool.

5.   (Optional)

- Rotate, zoom or pan your cropped photo. To help with the composition of your photo, see *Using the Rule of Thirds* on p.80.

- Adjust the frame to fit the crop—see below.

Adjusting frames

If a photo has been cropped inside a frame, you can adjust the size and shape of the frame to suit it. The frame can be, moved, rotated, resized and even recolored independent of the photo. You can even add an effect or color to the frame—without affecting the photo.

1. Select the framed photo with the ![Select tool icon] **Select** tool.

2. Click ![Select Frame Object icon] **Select Frame Object**.

3. To resize the frame, drag a handle. The frame's aspect ratio is preserved. To resize to any aspect ratio, hold down the **Shift** key while dragging.

4. (Optional) The **Select Frame Object** tool also lets you isolate the frame so you can add effects or change the frame's color—without affecting the photo inside it.

5. Click ⬅ **Back** to return to the ▲ **Select** tool.

Rotating, zooming, and panning

1. Select the photo, and then click the **Crop** button.

2. To rotate, or zoom into or out of the photo, click the buttons displayed at the right edge of the photo.

3. To pan the photo inside its frame, click and drag on the photo.

4. To use the **Rule of Thirds** to grid to help with your composition:

   ● On the Crop context toolbar, click ⊞ **Show/Hide Thirds Grid**.

   ● Click and drag on the photo to pan the image, positioning your main subject of interest at a point where any two lines intersect. (See *Using the Rule of Thirds Grid* on p. 80.)

5. To close the Crop window, click ↰ **Back**, or click elsewhere on the page or pasteboard area.

Replacing a framed photo

 Drag a photo from the **Photos** tab and drop it onto the frame. Digital Scrapbook Artist fits the photo to the frame automatically.

Deleting frames and framed photos

You can delete frames (along with the photos inside them) from your scrapbook pages. You can also remove frames from the **Frames** tab.

Deleting frames from the page

 Select a frame and press the **Delete** key.

If the frame contains a photo, this will also be deleted from the page.

Removing frames from the Frames tab

 On the **Frames** tab, select a frame and click its **Remove** button.

> This process will only remove frames from the **Photos** tab; it will not delete frames from your scrapbook pages.

Converting photos to frames

Photos you've added directly to your page (i.e., those that are not inside a decorative photo frame) can be converted so that they sit inside "frameless" frames.

Once converted, these frames function exactly like the decorative frames you've added from the **Frames** tab. For example, if you use the **AutoFlow** feature to automatically populate frames in your scrapbook, photos in frameless frames will also be replaced. (See *Using AutoFlow* on p. 114.)

> If you have used the Line tab to apply an outline or edge to your photo, when you convert the photo to a frame, the outline itself becomes the new frame. For

information on applying outline and edge effects, see *Changing line style* on p. 199 and the *Line tab* online Help topic.

To convert a photo to a frame:

1. Select the photo with the ![Select tool] **Select** tool.

2. On the context toolbar, click **Convert to Frame**.

   The photo is converted to a frame, and the ![Frame controls] Frame controls display beneath it.

   Notice also that the Photo context toolbar has been replaced with the Crop context toolbar.

You can now adjust the way your photo fits inside its frame by rotating, zooming, and panning. You can also crop the photo and adjust its frame to follow suit. See *Fitting photos to frames* on p. 113.

Creating your own photo frames

You can create your own Digikit photo frames using **the Frame Editor** dialog.

Once you've cut out your frame and placed it onto your page, simply drag a photo onto it—Digital Scrapbook Artist automatically fits the photo to the frame. All frames can be moved, resized, and rotated on the page. (See *Adding frames to the page* on p. 112.) You can also adjust the way your photo fits inside the frame by rotating, zooming, and panning. (See *Fitting photos to frames* on p. 113.)

Once you've created a Digikit photo frame, you can return to the **Frame Editor** dialog at any time to retouch its edges.

Creating your frame

1. On the Pages context toolbar, click ![icon] **Digikit Creator**. The **Digikit Creator** dialog opens.

2. Select the **Frames** category.

3. Click **Create Frame** and choose one of the following options:

    ● Select **Add Files**. In the **Open** dialog, browse to the folder containing the image you want to import, select the image and click **Open**. The image is automatically opened in the **Frame Editor** dialog.

    -or-

    ● Select **Add Folders**. In the **Open** dialog, browse to the folder containing the images you want to import and click **OK**. The first image in the folder is automatically opened in the Frame Editor dialog—when you've finished editing the next image in the folder will be opened.

4. Use the tools provided to cut out your frame. See the **Help** tab situated at the right of the **Frame Editor** dialog for detailed instructions.

5. When you have finished creating your frame in **Frame Editor**, click **OK** to save your frame.

    Your new frame will now be displayed in the **Frames** category of the **Digikit Creator**.

Retouching your frame

1. On the Pages context toolbar, click ![icon] **Digikit Creator**.

2. In the **Digikit Creator** dialog, select the **Frames** category.

3. Select the frame you want to retouch.

4. Click **Tweak**.

5. The frame opens in the **Frame Editor** dialog. Use the touch-up tools to refine your frame.

Working with text

Adding text

You can create artistic text and shape text in Digital Scrapbook Artist. Both text types are fully editable, and you can apply formatting, styles, and color fills before or after typing.

Text types overview

The following table outlines the main characteristics of artistic and shape text.

Text type	Use and characteristics
Artistic text 	<ul><li>Great for decorative typographic design.</li><li>Individual letters can be stretched, rotated, sheared, and combined with other items.</li></ul>

Shape text

- Lends itself well to blocks of body text where shape and flow contribute to the overall layout.

- Conforms to the containing shape. You can't manipulate individual letters, but you can achieve unique text flow effects by varying the container's properties.

- Does not have a line property.

Adding artistic text

1. On the Standard toolbar, click the 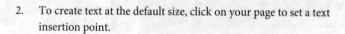 **Text** tool.

2. To create text at the default size, click on your page to set a text insertion point.

   - or -

   Click and drag on your page to set the size of the text insertion point.

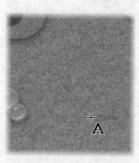

- To set text attributes before typing, adjust the settings on the Text context toolbar. (See *Formatting text* on p. 134.)

- To set text color before typing, set the **Line** and **Fill** swatches on the **Color** tab. (See *Changing line and fill color* on p. 225.)

3. Start typing. To start a new line of text, press the **Enter** key.

Adding shape text

1. Create a shape either from the QuickShape flyout or by closing a drawn line.

2. With the shape selected, start typing. Text flows within the shape and the **Text** tool is automatically selected.

 To set text attributes before typing, adjust the settings on the Text context toolbar. (See *Formatting text* on p. 134.)

 To set text color before typing, set the Line and Fill swatches on the Color tab. (See *Changing line and fill color* on p. 225.)

3. (Optional) To start a new line of text, press the **Enter** key.

- If you've typed more text into a shape than it can display, an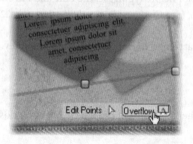
  Overflow button displays below the shape when it's selected.

To reveal all the text, enlarge the shape.

- or -

Click the [ ] **AutoFit** button on the Text context toolbar to
reduce the size of the text.

- To extract text from a shape (as an artistic text item), right-click the
  shape and click **Detach as New Item>Text**. To detach the text
  from its containing shape, simply drag it.

Working with text on the page

To select an entire artistic or shape text item:

- Click it with the [ ] **Select** tool.

To edit a text item:

1. Select the item with the [ ] **Select** tool, and then click the
   Edit button that displays below the item.

   - or -

Select the item with the **A Text** tool.

A text edit cursor is inserted inside the text.

2. Click and drag to select the text you want to edit, and then retype. See *Editing and deleting text* on p. 132.

To move a text item:

- Select it, and then drag it.

    - or -

    Click and drag its ✥ Move button.

To resize a text item:

- Select it and drag a corner resize handle.

To rotate a text item:

● Select it and drag its Rotate handle.

To apply text formatting:

● Select the text, and then adjust the settings on the Text context toolbar. See *Formatting text* on p. 134.

You can also rotate and shear text items, and apply shadows, transparency, and other effects. For details, see:

● Rotating and shearing items (p. 247)

● Adding drop shadows (p. 145)

● Applying transparency (p. 155)

● Adding outlines to text (p. 139)

● Applying 2D filter effects (p. 147)

Editing and deleting text

You can edit and delete artistic text and shape text directly on the page, or in the **Edit Text** dialog (for details on working in the **Edit Text** dialog, see online Help).

To edit text on the page:

1. Select the item with the  **Select** tool, and then click the **Edit** button that displays below the item.

    - or -

    Select the item with the  **Text** tool. A flashing text edit cursor is inserted inside the text.

2. Type new text at the insertion point, or click and drag to select the text you want to edit.

3. Type your new text.

To cut, copy, and paste text, use the standard Windows keyboard shortcuts.

To delete an entire text item:

1. Select a text item or shape with the **Select** tool.

2. Press the **Delete** key.

To delete selected characters or words:

1. Select a text item or shape with the **Select** tool.

2. Click the **Text** tool.

   A flashing text edit cursor is inserted inside the text.

3. Click and drag to select the text you want to delete, and then press the **Delete** key.

Formatting text

You can select and format artistic text and shape text directly on the page using the Text context toolbar, the **Format** menu, or the **Edit Text** dialog.

Selecting text for formatting

To format an entire text item:

1. Select the item with the  **Select** tool.

2. Use the Text context toolbar or **Format** menu to apply formatting, as described below.

To format selected letters or words:

1. Click the **A** **Text** tool, and then click and drag to select one or more characters or words.

2. Use the Text context toolbar or **Format** menu to apply formatting, as described below.

Using the Text context toolbar

The Text context toolbar lets you apply basic text attributes, such as point size, font style, alignment options, and so on, to selected text.

To format text from the Text context toolbar:

1.   Select a text item, a character, or a group of characters.

2.   On the Text context toolbar, adjust the settings described below:

- Select a font from the **Fonts** drop-down list.

  Lists font names and provides a preview of the selected text. Icons indicate the font type (e.g., **T** = TrueType).

- Select a text size from the **Point Size** drop-down list.

  Shows the height of the selected text in points.

- Click to apply bold, italic, or underline formatting.

- Click to apply left, center, right, or justified text alignment.

- Click to apply a bullet or numbered list style.

- Click to incrementally decrease or increase text indents.

- Click **AutoFit** to increase or decrease the size of shape text to fit its containing shape.

- Click to incrementally increase or decrease text size.

- Click to display the **Curved Text** flyout. Click a preset path to apply it to a selected artistic text item.

You can only fit artistic text to a curve.

Using the Format menu

1. Select a text item, a letter, or a group of letters.

2. On the **Format** menu, click **Character**, **Paragraph**, **Tabs**, **Bullets & Numbering**, or **Text Flow**.

3. Make your changes in the respective dialog(s), and then click **OK**.

See online Help for a detailed description of these options.

For special adjustments on artistic text:

1. Select the text item with the **Select** tool.

2. Click the ⌖ **Edit Points** button under the selected text.

Adjustment sliders and handles display above, to the left, and to the right of the text.

Hover the cursor over a slider to see its function.

- Drag the WRAPPING slider inward to change wrapping (how line wraps onto a new line).

- Drag the LEADING slider to change leading (space between lines).

- Drag the LETTER SPACING slider to change tracking (spacing between characters).

- To move a single character, select and drag the square handle at the character's lower-left corner.

To constrain movement horizontally or vertically, select a letter and then press and hold down the **Shift** key while dragging the letter.

- To move a group of letters, select them one at a time with the **Shift** key held down.

- To rotate a single character (illustrated), click its handle and drag the node on the opposite end of the displayed line to either side.

Adding outlines and edges to text

You can create interesting text effects by adding various line, brush stroke, and "fringed" edge styles to your artistic text items.

 You cannot apply lines and edges to shape text.

Adding outlines to artistic text

1. Select a text item with the **Select** tool.

2. Open the **Line** tab.

3. To apply a line style, click one of the following buttons:

Line tab button	Effect achieved
Solid	
Dash	

Line tab button	Effect achieved

 Double

 Calligraphic

4. Adjust the line width by dragging the slider.

 To remove an outline, click the **None** button.

Adding brush stroke edges to artistic text

1. Select a text item with the **Select** tool.

2. On the **Line** tab, click the **Stroke** button.

3. On the **Brushes** tab, select a brush stroke style.

The stroke is applied to the text outline.

4. Use the following **Line** tab controls to adjust the effect:

   - Change the stroke width by dragging the slider.

   - Increase or decrease the flow of the brush stroke by changing the brush **Flow** value.

Adding fringed edges to artistic text

1. Select a text item with the  **Select** tool.

2. On the **Line** tab, click the **Edge** button.

3. On the **Brushes** tab, select a brush stroke style.

4. Use the following **Line** tab controls to adjust the effect:

   - To apply the edge style *inside* the edge of the text, select the **Inner Edge** check box.

   - Change the stroke width by dragging the slider.

   - Increase/decrease the flow of the stroke by adjusting the **Flow**.

Adjusting the outline distance

Use the **Line** tab's **Offset** value to change the distance between a text item and its outline.

To adjust line offset:

1. Select a text item with the  **Select** tool.

2. On the **Line** tab, adjust the **Offset** value to achieve the desired effect.

   You can click the up/down arrow buttons; click the right arrow button and drag the slider; or type a value and press **Enter**.

Applying effects

8

Adding drop shadows

 When you **Start with a theme** via the Startup Wizard, preset drop shadow effects are selectable and available at the same time as you select embellishments, backgrounds, layouts, etc.

 Not all Digikits from the www.daisytrail.com shop come complete with ready-to-go drop shadow effects.

The 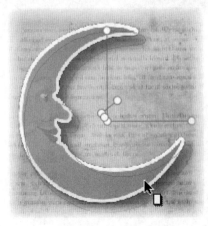 **Shadow Tool** is great for allowing freeform control of a drop shadow effect. With its on-the-page control nodes and supporting Shadow context toolbar, the tool offers various adjustments such as Opacity, Blur, and X (or Y) Shear.

Simple shadow
(drag from item center)

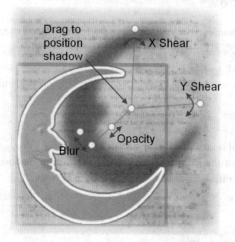

Offset shadow
(showing control nodes)

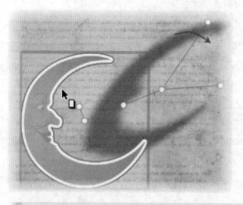

Skewed offset shadow
(adjusted X Shear)

Once you've created a basic shadow, you can further edit it as needed using the **Filter Effects** dialog.

Applying drop shadows with the Shadow Tool

1. Click the ▢ **Shadow Tool** on the **Standard** toolbar. Control nodes display to allow for shadow adjustment, as described in the annotated illustration above.

2. Drag across the item to create a drop shadow (note additional nodes being created).

3. Change blur, opacity, or shear properties by dragging the respective control nodes (or via the displayed context toolbar).

To change a shadow's color:

- Select the item, choose the **Shadow Tool**, then select a color from the **Color** tab.

To remove the shadow from an item:

- Double-click the item while the **Shadow Tool** is selected.

Applying other 2D filter effects

Changing material depth

If you've manipulated materials you've added to the page, perhaps by cutting out with the **Scissors** tool, you can apply some depth by applying an embossing effect.

On the **Effects** tab, adjust the **Material Depth** setting. (The greater the value, the more pronounced the embossed effect.)

Making feathered edges

Feathering applies a softer edge to scrapbook items such as embellishments or cut materials. The effect also looks great when applied to photo edges.

In the lower-right corner of the **Effects** tab, enter a **Feather Edge** value.

(This is the distance inside the item's outline from which feathering will be applied.)

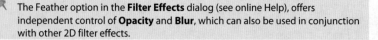

The Feather option in the **Filter Effects** dialog (see online Help), offers independent control of **Opacity** and **Blur**, which can also be used in conjunction with other 2D filter effects.

Applying filter effects

For more advanced control of filter effects, Digital Scrapbook Artist provides
a variety of **filter effects** that you can use to transform any item. The
following examples show each filter effect when applied to the letter "A".

Drop Shadow	Inner Shadow	Outer Glow	Inner Glow
Inner Bevel	Outer Bevel	Emboss	Pillow Emboss
Gaussian Blur	Zoom Blur	Radial Blur	Motion Blur
Color Fill	Feather	Outline	

You can also use the **Shadow Tool** to apply a shadow to an item directly on
your page. Control handles let you adjust shadow blur, opacity and color.

To apply 2D filter effects:

1. Select an item on your page and then click **Format>Filter Effects...**, or right-click the item and choose **Filter Effects...**

2. (Optional) By default, effects are applied directly to the selected object on the page.

    To view applied effects in a preview window, click ▷ **Show/Hide Preview** button. (This approach lets you work on your effects in isolation, without other page objects in view.)

3. To apply an effect, select its respective check box and then adjust the settings that display on the right.

    Adjust the sliders or enter specific values to vary the combined effect. (You can also select a slider and use the keyboard arrows.) Options differ from one effect to another.

4. (Optional) If you want the effect to remain fixed if you resize the item, clear the **Scale with object** check box. With the box selected, the effect's extent adjusts relative to any change in the item's size.

5. Click **OK** to apply the effect or **Cancel** to abandon changes.

Creating outlines

Digital Scrapbook Artist lets you create a colored outline around items, especially text and shapes (as a **filter effect**). For any outline, you can set the outline width, color fill, transparency, and blend mode. The outline can also take a gradient fill, a unique **contour** fill (fill runs from the inner to outer edge of the outline width), or pattern fill and can also sit inside, outside, or be centered on the item edge.

As with all effects you can switch the outline effect on and off. You'll be able to apply a combination of 2D or 3D filter effects along with your outline, by checking other options in the **Filter Effects** dialog.

Blur

Various blur effects can be applied to Digital Scrapbook Artist items. The types of blur include:

- **Gaussian**: the effect smoothes by averaging pixels using a weighted curve.

- **Zoom**: applies converging streaks to the image to simulate a zoom lens.

- **Radial**: applies concentric streaks to the item to simulate a rotating camera or subject.

- **Motion**: applies straight streaks to the item to simulate the effect of camera or subject movement.

Applying 3D filter effects

As well as 2D filter effects, Digital Scrapbook Artist provides a variety of **3D filter effects** that you can use to transform any item.

Such effects are selectable from the **Effects** tab, which offers an impressive choice of ready-to-go simulated natural and man-made surfaces. When applied to drawn items, previously "flat" appearances are brought to life by application of depth and texture.

The **Effects** tab displays a variety of thumbnail presets in various categories (Glass, Metal, Animals, etc.).

Click any thumbnail to apply it to the selected item.

💡 None of these 3D effects will "do" anything to an unfilled item—you'll need to have a fill there to see the difference they make!

Customizing 3D filter effects

Once an effect has been applied, you can customize it via a Filter Effects dialog.

1. Select the item with a 3D effect applied.

2. On the **Effects** tab, click *fx* **Filter Effects**.

3. In the **Filter Effects** dialog, you'll notice the **3D Effects** and **3D Lighting** boxes already selected.

4. Experiment with the effect by selecting various subcategories (e.g., 3D Bump Map, 2D Bump Map, etc.), and then adjusting the options on each pane.

You can also store an item's customized effect on the **Effects** tab to use later, as described in *Customizing gallery effects*, below.

Customizing gallery effects

Once you've customized an item's effect locally, you can add the effect to the **Effects** tab's gallery so that it will be available to use again. You can also delete effects from the gallery.

To add an item's effect to the gallery:

1. On the **Effects** tab, in the drop-down category list, select the category into which you want to add the effect.

2. Right-click the item with the effect applied and choose **Add To Effects...** (or choose this option from the **Format** menu).

3. Type a name for the effect and click **OK**.

   A new effect thumbnail displays in the currently displayed gallery category.

To delete an existing effect from the gallery:

- Right-click the effect's thumbnail and choose **Delete Design...**.

Paper textures

Paper textures simulate various real media textures of varying roughness and "feel", such as **Canvas**, **Cartridge**, **Embossed**, **Parchment**, and **Watercolor.**

As a paper texture is a layer property, the layer's texture is applied to all items on that layer.

A different texture can only be applied to a different layer (and to all its items).

Applying paper textures

1.   On the **Layers** tab, select the layer on which to apply a paper texture.

2.   Click the   **Paper Texture** button displayed after the chosen layer's name.

3.   In the **Bitmap Selector** dialog, select the **Paper Textures** category.

     A gallery of texture thumbnails displays.

4.   Choose a thumbnail and adjust **Scale** and **Opacity** values if required.

5.   Click **OK**.

     On the **Layers** tab, the layer's **Paper Texture** button changes to   ,
     indicating that a paper texture has been applied.

     All existing items on the layer, and any new items added to the layer,
     will adopt the applied paper texture.

Removing a paper texture

1.   On the **Layers** tab, locate the layer whose texture you want to remove
     and click the   **Paper Texture** button.

2.   In the **Bitmap Selector** dialog, click the **Remove** button. The paper
     texture is removed from all items on the layer.

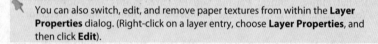

You can also switch, edit, and remove paper textures from within the **Layer Properties** dialog. (Right-click on a layer entry, choose **Layer Properties**, and then click **Edit**).

Applying transparency

Transparency effects are great for highlights, shading and shadows, and for simulating realism. They can make the critical difference between flat-looking illustrations and images with depth and snap.

Transparency may seem a bit tricky because you can't "see" it the way you can see a color fill applied to an item. In fact, it's there all the time in Digital Scrapbook Artist. Each new item has a transparency property: the default just happens to be "None"—that is, no transparency (opaque).

Transparencies work rather like fills that use "disappearing ink" instead of color. The more transparency in a particular spot, the more "disappearing" takes place there, and the more the item(s) underneath will show through.

Solid
(100% opaque)

Gradient
(100% to 0%
opaque)

Solid
(50% opaque)

Solid transparency distributes the transparency equally across the item. **Gradient** transparencies are created by drawing a path across the item; Linear transparencies are drawn by default but other categories such as **Radial**, **Ellipse**, **Conical**, **Plasma**, **Square**, **Three Points**, and **Four Points** can be created.

Applying solid transparency

The **Color** tab hosts a **Transparency** slider that controls the level of **solid** transparency applied to currently selected items.

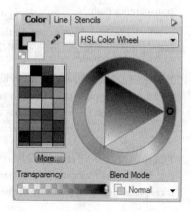

The further right the slider, the more opacity; the further left the more transparency. Remember that opacity is the inverse of transparency— 100% Opacity = 0% Transparency and vice versa.

To apply solid transparency from the Color tab:

1. With your item(s) selected, go to the **Color** tab.

2. Adjust the **Transparency** slider to set the level of transparency. The transparency is applied to the selected item(s) uniformly.

Applying gradient transparency

Just as a gradient fill can vary from light to dark, transparency can be applied as a opacity gradient, by drawing a gradient transparency path across the item (e.g., from 100% opacity to 0% opacity).

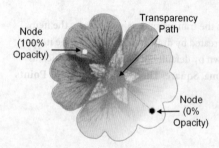

Transparency Path

Node (100% Opacity)

Node (0% Opacity)

For items with a gradient transparency applied, you can adjust the transparency effect by adding or subtracting nodes along the gradient transparency path.

The **Transparency Tool** displays an item's gradient transparency, indicated by two or more nodes situated along a path. You can reposition the nodes to adjust the transparency's starting point or end point.

For transparencies with multiple nodes, you can also adjust the intermediate levels of transparency. Each node has its own value, comparable to a key color in a gradient fill (see *Applying gradient fills* on p. 228). Each selected node's value can be altered directly on the page or in the Gradient Transparency Editor dialog.

To apply gradient transparency with Transparency Tool:

1. Select an item.

2. Click the **Transparency Tool** on the **Standard** toolbar.

3. To apply a simple Linear transparency (grading from 100% opacity to 0% opacity), click and drag across the item to define the transparency path.

    The effect starts where you place the start node, and ends where you place the end node.

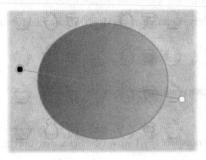

Changing transparency type

By default, the **Transparency Tool** applies a simple linear transparency on the drawn path. However, the tool's context toolbar lets you change to one of several transparency, e.g., Radial, Conical, Ellipse, Plasma, etc.

The path's appearance may change to reflect the transparency type, but the principles of editing the transparency path are the same.

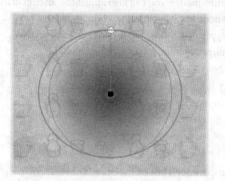

Editing gradient transparency

Once you've applied a gradient transparency, you can adjust its **path** on the item, and the **level** of transparency along the path. You can even create more complex transparency effects by adding extra nodes to the path and assigning different values to each node.

Each node along the path is selectable by clicking and can therefore adopt its own transparency value.

To adjust the transparency path:

1. Select the item with a gradient transparency applied.

2. Click the ⚱ **Transparency Tool** on the **Standard** toolbar.

3. Drag the displayed nodes to new positions. You'll notice the effect change as you drag a node.

Editing a **gradient transparency** path is similar to editing a solid gradient fill path (see *Editing gradient fills* on p. 232). Adding a level of transparency means varying the transparency gradient by introducing a new **node**, and assigning the node a particular value. For transparencies with multiple nodes, each node has its own value, comparable to a key color in a gradient fill.

You can either edit the path directly using the **Transparency Tool**, or use the Gradient Transparency Editor dialog (similar to the Gradient Fill Editor). Both methods let you define key values along the path.

The **Gradient Transparency Editor** dialog lets you fine-tune the actual spread of transparency between pairs of key values, and displays the transparency gradient, with pointers marking the nodes (corresponding to nodes on the path) that define specific transparency values. Again, black represents 100% opacity, and white represents 0% opacity, with grayscale values in between. A sample window at the lower right shows the overall transparency effect.

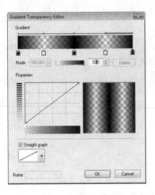

For details of how to edit and manage transparency in the **Gradient Transparency Editor** dialog, see online Help.

To edit gradient transparency directly:

1. Select the item, then the  **Transparency Tool** button from the Standard toolbar. The item's transparency path appears, with start and end nodes.

2. To add a transparency node, hover over the path until the cursor changes then click on the point on the path where you want to add the node.

3. To change the grayscale/transparency value of any existing node, including the start and end nodes, select the node and move the Color tab's transparency slider to the required value.

4. To move a node you've added, simply drag it to a new position along the transparency path.

5. To delete a node you've added, select it and press **Delete**.

Cutting, cropping, and erasing

Cutting items

Use the **Scissors** tool to cut any item or group of items on your page. For example, you might want to cut a material or embellishment, or add a decorative cut edge to a photograph.

You can cut freeform shapes, or apply a preset "punch" shape.

Cutting freeform shapes

1. Use the **Select** tool to select one or more items.

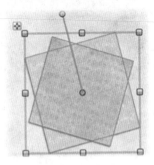

To cut through selected items on multiple layers, ensure that the **Edit All Layers** button, on the **Layers** tab, is selected. (See *Working with layers* in online Help .)

2. On the **Standard** toolbar, click the **Scissors** tool.

3. On the Scissors context toolbar, select a scissor type from the drop-down list.

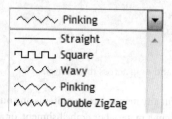

4. Optional:

   ○ To adjust the regularity of the freeform cutting line, adjust the **Smoothness** setting. To do this, click the up and down arrows, or click the right arrow and drag the slider.

   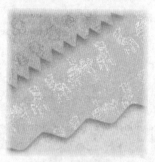

   ○ To adjust the length of each unit of the cutting edge, change the **Wavelength** setting.

To adjust the depth of each unit of the cutting edge, change the **Amplitude** setting.

 You can't adjust wavelength or amplitude for **Straight** cutting lines.

5. To create a freeform cut, click and drag across the item(s).

 Unselected items that the cutting line crosses will not be split.

6. To remove a cut section, click it.

- or -

To retain a cut section, hold down the **Shift** key, and then click the section you want to retain. (All other portions of the item will be deleted.)

- or -

To retain both sections and split them apart:

- Click the 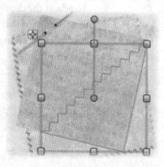 **Select** tool and then click a cut section.

- Drag the section into its new position.

Punching shapes

1. Use the **Select** tool to select one or more items.

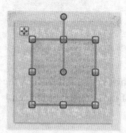

2. On the Standard toolbar, click the **Scissors** tool.

3. On the Scissors context toolbar, select a scissor type from the drop-down list.

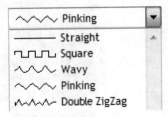

4. Click to expand the **Punches** flyout, and then click a preset punch shape to apply it to your item.

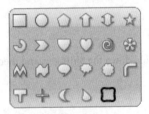

5. The punch is applied to the item. Click the **Cut** button that displays below the item.

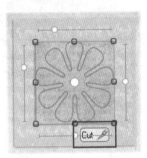

6. To delete or retain cut sections:

● To delete a cut section, click it.

● To retain a cut section, hold down the **Shift** key, and then click the section.

- To retain both sections and split them apart, click
  the **Select** tool, then click a cut section and drag it into its new
  position.

Combining, cropping, and joining items

Digital Scrapbook Artist provides the powerful **Combine**, **Crop**, and **Join**
(**Add**, **Subtract**, and **Intersect**) commands, which you can use on multiple
selections to create new shapes.

For easy access to these commands, use the buttons on **Arrange** tab.

Combining items

Combining merges selected items into a composite item, with a hole where
filled regions overlap. The composite takes the line and fill of the bottom
item.

1. Use the  **Select** tool to create a multiple selection containing the items to be combined.

2. On the **Arrange** tab, click the **Combine** button. The composite takes the line and fill of the back item.

 To break apart the item, select it and click the button again.

 You can also use the **Crop** tool to crop photos and other items on your page. See *Cropping photos* on p. 171.

Cropping items

1. Use the  **Select** tool to create a multiple selection containing the items to be cropped.

2. On the **Arrange** tab, click the **Crop** button to display a flyout.

3. To crop the bottom item to the outline of the top item, select **Crop to Top**.

- or -

To crop the top item to the outline of the bottom item, click **Crop to Bottom**.

To remove the crop, click **Arrange>Crop>Uncrop**.

Clipping items

1. Use the **Select** tool to create a multiple selection containing the items to be clipped.

2. On the **Arrange** tab, click the down arrow to expand the Crop flyout.

3. To clip the bottom item to the outline of the top item, click **Clip to Top**.

- or -

To clip the top item to the outline of the bottom item, click **Clip to Bottom**.

To remove the clip, click **Arrange>Crop>Uncrop**.

Adding items

Adding creates a new item that's the sum of two or more selected items, whether or not they overlap.

1. Use the ![Select tool] **Select** tool to create a multiple selection of items. (The items need not overlap.)

2. On the **Arrange** tab, click ![Add icon] **Add**.

   The new item is a composite of the selected items, taking the line and fill of the bottom item.

Subtracting items

Subtracting creates a new item, retaining only the portion of the bottom item that is not overlapped.

This command is particularly useful for cutting out shapes from photos.

1.   Use the ![Select tool]   **Select** tool to create a multiple selection of overlapping items.

(The items must overlap.)

2. On the **Arrange** tab, click  **Subtract**.

The new item consists of the non-overlapping portion(s) of the bottom selected item.

Intersecting items

Intersecting creates a new item, retaining the overlap and discarding the rest.

1. Use the  **Select** tool to select two overlapping items.

2. On the **Arrange** tab, click  **Intersect**.

The new item consists of the overlapping portions of the previously selected items, taking the line and fill of the back item.

 Add, **Subtract**, and **Intersect** produce a permanent new item out of any selected items. You can only break the resulting item apart *immediately* after creating it by clicking the **Undo** button on the **Standard** toolbar.

Erasing and adding to items

Erasing   Adding to

Digital Scrapbook Artist provides the following tools for erasing and adding to existing lines and shapes.

 Erase Tool

Lets you erase portions of a selected item or items. You can control the extent of erasing by setting eraser tip width and pressure (if using a graphics tablet).

 You can erase on an individual layer or across multiple layers. (See *Working with layers* in online Help.)

Freeform Paint Tool

Lets you add to or 'grow' the boundary of an existing shape or line—useful for reshaping existing items, or for creating unusual filled shapes.

 If you add to or erase from a bitmap, QuickShape, or artistic text item, the item will be converted to curves, preventing further editing in their original form.

Erasing portions of an item

1. Use the **Select** tool to select an item.

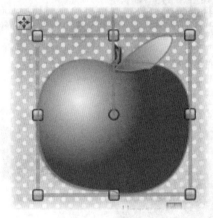

2. On the **Standard** toolbar, click the **Erase Tool**.

3. On the context toolbar, choose an eraser tip shape.

4. (Optional) Set the tip width by adjusting the **Width** value.

5. Position the cursor, and drag over the item's edge. The area to be erased is drawn temporarily (use the **Ctrl** key to redefine the erase area while drawing).

6. Release the mouse button to erase the area drawn.

The erasing process shows the background color belonging to any item behind it (either on the same layer or a layer below the current layer).

Adding to an item

1. Use the **Select** tool to select an item.

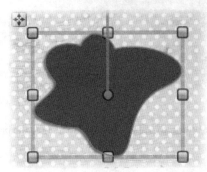

2. On the **Standard** toolbar, click the **Freeform Paint Tool**.

3. On the context toolbar, choose a shape for the tool's tip.

4. (Optional):

    ◦ Set the tip width by adjusting the **Width** value.

    ◦ To create a series of shapes without switching tools, click to disable the **Select-on-Create** button.

5. Position the cursor over the item and drag over an item boundary.

    You'll see blue shading, which represents the area to be added.

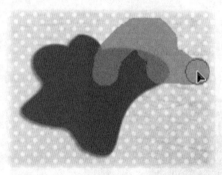

6.   Release the mouse button to reshape the item to include the painted area.

Adding lines, shapes, and stencils

10

Adding lines, shapes, and stencils

Using QuickShapes

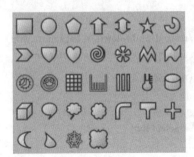

The QuickShapes flyout provides a variety of commonly used shapes that you can instantly add to your page.

To create a QuickShape:

1. Click **Shapes** on the **Standard** toolbar and select a shape from the flyout.

2. On your page, either:

   - Double-click to place a default-sized QuickShape.

     -or-

   - Click and drag to draw your QuickShape at a specific size. To constrain the aspect ratio (for example, to obtain a square or circle), hold down the **Shift** key while dragging.

> New QuickShapes adopt the currently set line and fill, as defined on the Color tab. See *Changing fill and line color* on p. 225.

Once you've drawn your QuickShape, you can adjust its properties—for example, apply solid fills (p. 225), gradient fills (p. 228), or transparency effects (p. 155). You can even use sliding **control handles** to create variations on the original QuickShape.

You can also use the QuickShape context toolbar, situated above the workspace, to swap QuickShapes and adjust line weight, color, style, and more.

All QuickShapes can be positioned, resized, and rotated. What's more, you can adjust their appearance as soon as they are drawn, or at a later time.

To adjust the appearance of a QuickShape:

1.   Select the item with the ![Select tool cursor] **Select** tool.

2.   Click the ![Edit button] **Edit** button displayed beneath the item. This reveals sliding round handles around the shape. (Different QuickShapes have different handles.)

3.   Drag the handle to change the appearance of a QuickShape.

For example, dragging the top sliding handle to the right on the QuickStar below will produce a very different star shape.

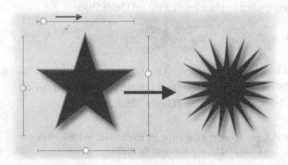

Drawing lines and shapes

You can draw straight or curved lines. As soon as you draw a line you'll see its **points** appear. The line between any two points is called a **line segment**. Freeform and curved lines usually have many points; straight lines have only two.

All lines and line segments have **line properties** such as **color** and **weight** (thickness). For details on applying color to lines and shapes, see *Changing line and fill color* on p. 225.

When a line, or series of line segments, forms a complete, enclosed outline, it becomes a new **closed** item called a **shape**. Because shapes can be filled with a solid or gradient fill, they have **fill properties** as well as line properties.

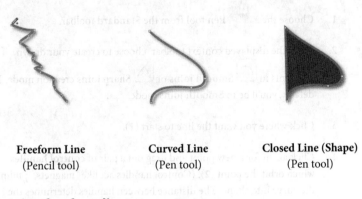

| **Freeform Line** | **Curved Line** | **Closed Line (Shape)** |
| (Pencil tool) | (Pen tool) | (Pen tool) |

Drawing freeform lines

1. Click the 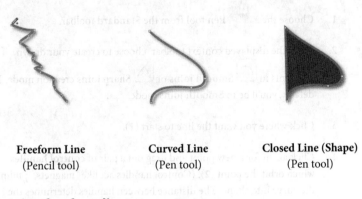 **Pencil** tool on the **Standard** toolbar.

2. Click once, then drag across the page, drawing a line as you go. The line appears immediately and follows your mouse movements.

   💡 To draw a straight line, hold down the **Shift** key down as you drag.

3. To end the line, release the mouse button. The line will automatically smooth out using a minimal number of points. Note the dots indicating its points—at each end, and at each point where two line segments meet.

4. (Optional) To set the degree of smoothing to be applied to the line (and subsequent lines), set the **Smoothness** value on the context toolbar.

Drawing curved lines

Curved lines are created as a series of connected line segments (which may be curved or straight) using a series of "connect the dots" mouse clicks. New line segments are added all the time. The tool is designed for drawing complex, combination curves and shapes in a highly controlled way.

1. Choose the ![pen] **Pen** tool from the **Standard** toolbar.

2. From the displayed context toolbar, choose to create your drawn segments in ![smooth] **Smooth joins** or ![sharp] **Sharp joins** creation mode. By default, you'll be in **Smooth joins** mode.

3. Click where you want the line to start (**1**).

4. Click again for a new point and drag out a pair of **control handles** which orbit the point (**2**). (Control handles act like "magnets," pulling the curve into shape. The distance between handles determines the depth of the resulting curved line.) Release the mouse button to create your curve segment (**3**).

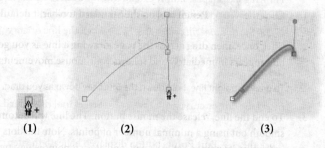

(1)　　　　　　　(2)　　　　　　　(3)

To extend an existing line, click beyond the end of your current curve to create a new point (thus creating another curve segment).

Normally, curve segments end in a symmetric (evenly rounded) corner (**4**), with control handles locked together.

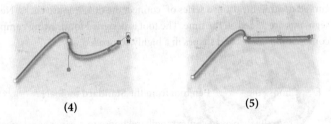

(**4**)   (**5**)

However, you can press the **Alt** key while drawing the segment to define a "cusp" or sharp corner (**5**). This locks the control handle on the last created point. For more on line corners, see *Editing lines and shapes* on p. 188.

5.   To end the line, press **Esc** or choose a different tool.

Drawing shapes

To close a freeform line or curve as you draw:

●   For irregular shapes, simply extend the line back to its starting point. Shapes have an interior which is filled with the current **default fill** (see *Changing line and fill colors* on p. 225) when the line or curve is closed.

To close an existing line or curve (with a straight line):

1.   Select the line or curve with the   **Select** tool (**Standard** toolbar).

2.   Click the   **Edit Points** button displayed beneath the item.

3.   Select   **Close Curve** button on the context toolbar. A Straight segment appears, closing the curve.

If you're trying to draw a cartoon outline made up of many independent curves (e.g., a cartoon ear, rose, etc.) you may want to fill each curve without closing it. This is made easy by using the **Fill-on-Create** feature.

To fill an unclosed curve automatically:

- Select the **Pencil**, **Pen**, or **Brush** tool (**Standard** toolbar).

- On the context toolbar, click to enable Fill-on-Create, and then select a fill from the **Color** tab.

  You'll also need to ensure Select-on-Create is enabled on the context toolbar.

- Draw a freeform line into a curve. The resulting curve is closed automatically and filled with the current fill color.

Editing lines and shapes

All items, lines, and shapes are composed of one or more **line segments** (which can be straight or curved) that are joined at their **points**.

To edit a line or shape, you can manipulate its segments and/or points, redraw lines, reshape lines (by moving or adding/deleting points), or join two or more lines together.

To:	Do this:
Move a whole line	Using any selection tool, drag the line.
Redraw part of a line	Draw a new portion with the **Pencil** tool while in **Editing** mode.
Extend a line	Drag away from a node, creating a new segment.
Reshape a line (or curve)	Drag points while in **Editing** mode.
Simplify a line (remove points)	Adjust the **Smoothness** setting on the **Pencil** tool's context toolbar.
	Select and delete points while in **Editing** mode.
	Use Clean Curves to remove unwanted points.
Enhance a line (add points)	Click anywhere on a line segment while in **Editing** mode.
Change the type of point or line segment	While in **Editing** mode, select a point then pick a different segment from the context toolbar.
Convert to straight line segments	Click the **Straighten Line** or **Convert to Straight Lines** buttons (Context toolbar).

To:	Do this:

Adjust a shape

- Drag points while in **Editing** mode, and/or adjust control handles.

- Use the context toolbar to break open the shape, then add line segments.

Join two lines together

- Select two lines, then choose **Join Curves** from the **Tools** menu.

Redrawing part of a line

You can use the **Pencil** tool to redraw any portion of a line or curve.

To redraw part of a selected line:

1. Select the line, then the  **Pencil** tool. Hover the displayed cursor over the line, at the point where you want to begin redrawing.

    The cursor changes to indicate you can begin drawing.

2. Click on the line.

3. Keep the mouse button down and drag to draw a new line section, connecting it back to another point on the original line. Again, the cursor changes to include a curve when you're close enough to the line to make a connection.

When you release the mouse button, the original portion is replaced by the newly drawn portion.

Extending lines

Any kind of open line (that is, one that hasn't been closed to create a shape) can be resized. You can use any of the line tools to do so.

To extend a line:

1. Select the drawn line with the  **Select** tool, and then select the line's drawing tool.

2. Move the cursor over either of the end points, a small + cursor will appear. Click at that location.

3. Drag out to draw a freeform line beyond the end point.

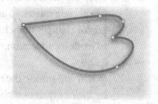

4. The line that you create will be a continuation of the existing line, as a new line segment.

5. You can optionally close the curve, creating a new shape that can take a fill!

Reshaping lines

To reshape a line, you can drag or adjust its points and segments.

To reshape a straight line segment, first convert it to curves (see *Converting a shape to editable curves* in online Help).

To reshape a curved line:

1. Select the line with the **Select** tool.

2. Click the ▷ **Edit Points** button displayed beneath the item. The line's points appear, and a context toolbar displays. (Some of the toolbar's buttons may be 'grayed out.' These will become available when you select a point or part of the line/shape to work on.)

3. Either:

   • Hover over a segment and drag the segment to form a new curve shape.

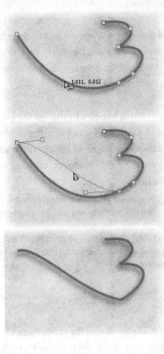

-or-

• Hover over a point (the 🖑 cursor will display) and click to select the point. Optionally, **Shift**-click or drag out a marquee to select multiple points.

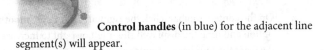

Control handles (in blue) for the adjacent line segment(s) will appear.

Note that each segment in the line has a control handle at either end, so when you select an **end point** or **interior point**, you'll see either a control handle on each selected end point (one segment) or a pair of handles at a selected interior point (two segments), respectively.

Drag any selected point to reshape adjacent segment(s). All selected points move in the same direction, so you can reshape the curve by selecting specific points. (**Shift**-drag to constrain the movement to horizontal or vertical.)

Drag one or more control handles to change the curvature of the line on either side of a point. You can shorten or lengthen the handles, which changes the depth of the **curve**, or alter the handle angle, which changes the curve's **slope**.

 By changing the type of point you can change how the adjacent segments behave. (See *Changing points and line segments*, below.)

 As a shortcut when selecting points, you can press **Tab** or **Shift-Tab** to select the next or previous point along the line (following the order in which points were created).

Simplifying or enhancing lines and shapes

The more points there are on a line or shape, the more control over its shape you have. The fewer points there are, the simpler (smoother) the line or shape. You can adjust smoothness to refine the curve most recently drawn (as long as the line is still selected).

To adjust the smoothness of the most recent pencil line:

1. Click the **Pencil** tool and draw a freeform line.

2. On the context toolbar, click the right arrow on the **Smoothness** option and drag the displayed slider left or right to increase or decrease the number of points (you can also type absolute values into the input box).

   The line is made less complex, i.e., smoother, by dragging the slider to the right to decrease the number of points.

To add a point to a line or curve:

● If the line is selected with the drawing tool used to create it, single-click (for a pen line) or double-click (for a pencil line) on the line to add a new point.

- or -

● If the line is not selected, select it with the [cursor icon] **Select** tool, click [arrow icon] **Edit Points**, and then single-click on the line to add a new point.

The new point is created and selected by default.

To delete a point:

1. Select the line with the [cursor icon] **Select** tool, and click [arrow icon] **Edit Points**.

- or -

Select the line with the [pen icon] **Pen** tool.

2. On the context toolbar, click [icon] **Delete Point** (or press the **Delete** key).

You can also reposition the points, and reshape the line or shape, by dragging on its control handles (see below).

If you've converted a shape to curves you can clean up unwanted points by using the **Clean Curves** command. (See *Converting a shape to editable curves* in online Help.)

Changing points and line segments

Each segment in a line has a control handle at either end, so at each interior or "corner" point (where two segments join) you'll see a pair of handles.

The behavior of these handles—and the curvature of the segments on either side—depends on whether the point is set to be **sharp**, **smooth**, **symmetric**, or **smart**. You can quickly identify a point's type by selecting it and then checking to see which button is selected on the displayed context toolbar.

Each type's control handles behave differently as illustrated in the table below.

To change one or more points to a different type:

1. Select the item with the **Select** tool.

2. Click the **Edit Points** button displayed beneath the item, then click on the point you want to change (**Shift**-click or drag out a marquee to select multiple points).

3. Click one of the point buttons on the displayed context toolbar:

 A **Sharp Corner** means that the line segments on either side of the point are completely independent. The corner can be quite pointed.

 A **Smooth Corner** means that the slope of the line is the same on both sides of the point, but the depth of the two joined segments can be different.

 At a **Symmetric Corner**, points join line segments with the same slope and depth on both sides of the point.

> Normally, custom segments you draw with the Pen tool end in a symmetric corner.

 Smart Corner points automatically determine slope and depth for a rounded, best-fitting curve.

> If you attempt to adjust a smart corner's handles, it changes to a smooth corner. You can always reset the point—but to maintain smart points, be careful what you click on!

You can also use the context toolbar to define a line segment as either straight or curved.

To change a line segment from straight to curved, or vice versa:

1. While in Editing mode, select the leading point of the line segment (the point nearer the start of the line).

2. Then, either:

   - To make a line segment straight, click [image] **Straighten Line** on the context toolbar. The selected segment immediately jumps to a straight line.
     -or-

   - To make a line segment curved, click one of the point buttons (describe above) on the context toolbar: **Sharp Corner**, **Smooth Corner**, **Symmetric Corner**, or **Smart Corner**. You can then adjust the curvature of the newly created curved segment.

To convert to straight lines:

1. While in Editing mode, select the curve.

2. On the context toolbar, choose [image] **Convert to Straight Lines**. The curve segments are replaced by straight line segments throughout the line.

Adjusting a shape

As described previously, you can easily turn a curve into a shape by connecting its end points. You can go the other way, too—break open a shape in order to add one or more line segments.

To break open a line or shape:

1. Select the item with the [image] **Select** tool.

2.   Click the ⬐ **Edit Points** button displayed beneath the item.

3.   Select the point on the closed curve where you want the break to occur.

4.   Click the **Break Curve** button on the context toolbar so that the line will separate. A shape will become a line, with the selected point split into two points, one at each end of the new line.

5.   You can now reposition the points and reshape the line by dragging on the handles.

> When you first break a curve the two points are in exactly the same location and so the curve may still look as if it is connected. If you drag one of the red point ends away you will quickly see the separation.

> If the broken shape had a fill you can change the unwanted fill to be transparent by using the Color tab's Fill swatch.

Joining lines

You can connect any two straight or curved lines to form a new line.

To join two lines together:

1.   Select both lines by **Shift**-clicking with the **Select** tool.

2.   Choose **Join Curves** from the **Tools** menu. The end control point of one line is connected with the start control point of the other.

Changing line style

All lines, including those that enclose shapes, have numerous properties, including color, style, line ends, weight, join, and cap.

Using the Line tab, you can adjust **plain line** properties for any freeform, straight, or curved line, as well as for the outline of a shape or photo.

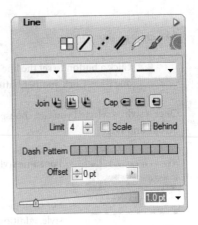

Changing line color

The color swatches selected from your themed Digikit become available in the **Color** tab. For details on adding or editing plain line colors, see *Changing line and fill color* on p. 225.

Changing line style

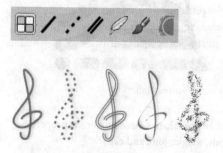

A series of buttons arranged along the top of the **Line** tab set the line style.

Solid, **Dash**, **Double**, **Calligraphic**, and **Stroke** styles can be applied.

A fringed **Edge** style can also be applied to shapes, text, and photo edges.

To change line style:

- Click a button to set the line style—only one style can be set at any one time. Click another button to jump to that style.

Once a style is selected you can choose line ends for most styles (except **Stroke** and **Edge**).

For some styles, variations are also available.

For example, for a [icon] **Dash** or [icon] **Double** line style, additional dash patterns (below) and double line options can be selected.

To select a line end:

- From the 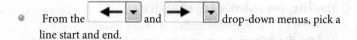 and drop-down menus, pick a line start and end.

Other styles such as **Dash** and **Calligraphic** offer further customization of the chosen style.

Two styles, **Stroke** and **Edge**, let you apply a brush, chosen from the Brushes tab, to the edge of a shape or edge. You'll see your current brush shown on the **Line** tab. Both styles look great when applied to artistic text. (See *Adding outlines and edges to text* on p. 139.)

For changing line caps and ends, see online Help.

Changing line width

On a selected line, curve, or shape, drag the **Weight** slider on the **Line** tab.

To turn off the line, set the value to 0.0pt.

Copying an item's formatting

Use **Format Painter** to copy an item's line and fill properties directly to
another item (you can even copy between line/shape and text items).

💡 The Format Painter is particularly useful if you've taken the time to fine-tune
an item's appearance (e.g., you may have applied a complex fill or
combination of filter effects), and want to apply the same format to other
items in your scrapbook.

To apply an item's formatting to another:

1. Select the item whose formatting you wish to copy.

2. Click 🖌 **Format Painter** on the **Standard** toolbar. When you click
    the button, the selected item's formatting is "picked up."

3. Click the item to which you want to apply the "picked up" formatting.
    The second item becomes selected and the formatting is applied.

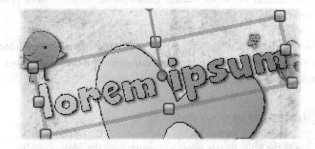

- To cancel Format Painter mode, press **Esc**, click on a blank area of the page, or click any other tool button.

- While in Format Painter mode, to select an item *without* pasting formatting, hold down the **Shift** key and then select the item.

- When copying formatting from one text item to another, text properties such as font and style are also passed along.

Using stencils

The **Stencils** tab provides a selection of ready-to-go, fun stencils that will add impact to any scrapbook page. Whether you paint over them with the **Brush**

tool, or use them to cut out a design from a photo, stencils provide endless opportunities for creativity.

If you're feeling really creative, you can add your own stencils to the **Stencils** tab! You can also add new folders and categories in which to save your stencils.

Adding stencils to your page

1. On the **Stencils** tab, select a category from the drop-down list.

   The lower gallery displays thumbnails of the stencils available in the selected category.

2. Click and drag a thumbnail from the gallery onto your page.

Painting over stencils

1. Click the  **Brush** tool.

2. Choose a brush type from the **Brushes** tab and set your brush color on the Color tab. (See *Adding brush strokes* on p. 209.)

   💡 Brushes in the **Airbrushes** and **Natural Media** categories are particularly suited to stencil work.

3. Paint over the stencil with your chosen brush.

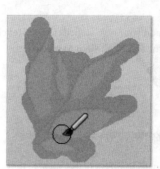

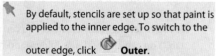

By default, stencils are set up so that paint is applied to the inner edge. To switch to the outer edge, click **Outer**.

4. Click **Lift Stencil** to remove the stencil and reveal the painted design beneath it.

Cutting out a stencil from a photo

1. Drag a photo from the **Photos** tab and drop it on top of your stencil.

2. Position the photo so that it displays as required inside the stencil outline.

3. Select the stencil and click  **Lift Stencil** to remove the stencil and reveal the cut out design beneath it.

Creating your own stencils

You can create a stencil from any item on your page—embellishments, frames, and letters work particularly well.

To create your own stencil:

● Simply drag an item from your scrapbook page and drop it onto the **Stencils** tab.

Working with categories and folders

You can create your own categories and folders in which to store your stencils.

To create a new stencil category:

1. (Optional) To create the new category inside a folder you have previously created (see below), select the folder from the upper drop-down list.

2. Click the ▷ **Stencils Tab Menu** button and click **Add Category...**

3. Type a name for your new category.

4. Click **OK**.

To create a new folder:

1. Click the ▷ **Stencils Tab Menu** button and click **Add Folder...**

2. Type a name for your new folder and click **OK**.

To rename a category or folder:

1. On the **Stencils** tab, in the drop-down list, select the category/folder you want to rename.

2. Click the ▷ **Stencils Tab Menu** button and click **Rename Category/Folder**.

3. Type the new name and click **OK**.

To delete a category or folder:

1.   On the **Stencils** tab, in the drop-down list, select the category/folder
     you want to delete.

2.   Click the ▷ **Stencils Tab Menu** button and click **Delete
     Category/Folder**.

⚠   All stencils contained in the selected category/folder will also be deleted.

Adding brush strokes

11

Adding brush strokes

 Add artistic flair to your scrapbooks with the **Brush** tool.

The **Brushes** tab provides a wide range of brushes. Choose from preset, categorized **Global** brushes, or add themed **Digikit** brushes to your workspace. If you're feeling really creative, you can even create your own custom brushes. (For information on creating and customizing brushes, see online Help.)

You can draw and paint with your mouse or with a pen tablet. The tablet's pressure-sensitive pen tip allows control of stroke width or transparency (see *Pressure sensitivity* in online Help).

Choosing brush types

Brush types

The **Brushes** tab's **Global** category provides the following natural stroke and spray brushes:

- **Airbrushes**
  Add dramatic, soft, or textured airbrush effects.

- **Edges**
  Apply inner or outer edge effects to any shape.

- **Embroidery**
  'Stitch' items to your page with these colorful brushes.

- **Flowers**
  Paint your pages with flower and leaf spray brushes.

- **Fun & Celebrations**
  Create cheerful, fun layouts with confetti, sweets, stardust, and clouds.

○ **Glitter**
Make your pages sparkle with glitter dust and glitter glue brushes.

○ **Grunge**
Add aged and grunge effects to your layouts.

○ **Natural Media**
Apply paint, charcoal, pencil, pen, and other natural media brush strokes.

○ **Photo**
Add realistic lace, rope, ribbon, and rope effects with this collection of photo brushes.

○ **Special Effects**
Paint with bubbles, fire, snowflakes, and more!

Selecting brushes from the Brushes tab

The **Brushes** tab lets you view brushes currently being used in your scrapbook, and serves as a container for supplied brush presets, themed Digikit brushes, and your own brush designs.

The **Document** category shows the brush types used in the currently active scrapbook.

This category is useful for 'bookmarking' brushes for easy reuse.

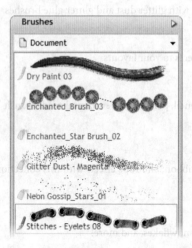

The **Global** category stores the supplied brush presets under a series of pre-defined subcategories.

You can add, rename and reorder any category and even create nested categories within categories.

These brushes are available to all scrapbooks currently open.

The **Digikit** category displays the themed brushes added from the **Digikit Browser**.

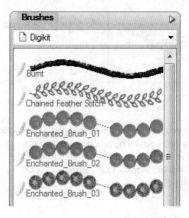

See *Adding brushes from Digikits*, below.

Adding brushes from Digikits

1. On the Pages context toolbar, click **Add items from Digikits**. The **Digikit Browser** dialog opens.

2. In the **Digikit Browser**, select the Digikit from which you want to add brushes.

3. Scroll to the **Brushes** category, and then click to select the brush(es) you want to use. To add all brushes from the Digikit, click **Add All Items**.

 If you select a brush from a featured free or purchasable Digikit—the **Digikit Not Installed** dialog will display and you will be prompted to visit the DaisyTrail.com shop. Once you've installed your free or purchased Digikit, the brush will be added to the **Digikit** category of the **Brushes** tab on selection. (See *Buying Digikits* on p. 54.)

4. (Optional) Click ⬅ **Back to 'All Digikits'** to add brushes from other Digikits.

5. When you've finished selecting brushes, click **Done**.

If you're creating your own brushes you can create your own brush categories by right-clicking on the tab's **Category** drop-down menu.

Creating brush strokes

You can apply brush strokes directly to the page using your mouse or pen tablet. If you're using a pen tablet, you can control stroke width and transparency by adjusting pressure sensitivity (see *Pressure sensitivity* in online Help).

Applying brush strokes

1. On the **Standard** toolbar, click the **Brush** tool.

The Brush cursor indicates that the Brush is selected and that you're ready to paint.

2. On the **Brushes** tab, choose a brush category from the drop-down list, and then select a brush stroke style from the gallery.

   At the top of the workspace, notice that the Brush context toolbar is displayed. Use the controls on this toolbar to set the properties of your brush stroke, as described in steps 3 to 6 below.

The following steps provide an overview of the brush properties. For more details, see *Setting brush stroke properties* on p. 219.

3. Click the **Color** button and select a brush stroke color using the **Color Picker** dialog.

4. Set the **Width**, **Opacity**, and **Smoothness** of your brush stroke.

   Click the up and down arrows, or click the right arrow and then drag the slider (as shown for smoothness, opposite).

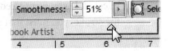

5.   (Optional) If you want to fill your closed or unclosed shape as you paint (see illustration below):

Enable the
Fill-on-Create button, and then set the Fill swatch on the **Color** tab.

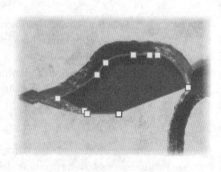

6.   (Optional) If you want to be able to edit your strokes immediately after painting them, enable the **Select-on-Create** button.

7.   With the brush cursor drag a brush stroke across your page.

The properties currently defined on the Brush context toolbar settings will be adopted for subsequent brush strokes.

8.   After this first brush stroke, there are two ways in which you can paint subsequently, depending on whether you have enabled the **Select-on-Create** option.

● **Edit, then paint**

If **Select-on-Create** is not enabled, when you release the mouse button, the stroke you just created is not selected. If you want to edit or add to the stroke, you must first select it.

Use this method when you're happy to set all your brush stroke properties *before* painting—and particularly if you intend to paint repeatedly with the same brush stroke style.

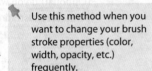

- **Paint and edit**

  If **Select-on-Create** is enabled, when you release the mouse button, the stroke you just created is automatically selected, allowing you to add to or edit it immediately.

 Use this method when you want to change your brush stroke properties (color, width, opacity, etc.) frequently.

Press the **Esc** key to deselect the current brush stroke.

A brush stroke can be extended or reshaped, as for a straight or curved line (see *Editing lines and shapes* in online Help). The brush stroke path can also be reversed, closed, or opened.

Setting brush stroke properties

You can set the properties of your brush strokes (both before and after creating them) using the Brush context toolbar.

To set brush stroke properties:

1. To set properties before painting, click the **Brush** tool and choose a brush style from the Brushes tab.

   - or -

   To set properties of an existing brush stroke, select the stroke.

   The Brush context toolbar displays.

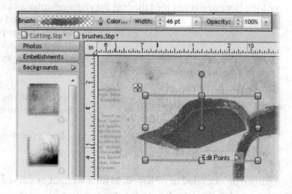

2. To change the brush design, select a category on the **Brushes** tab.

3. To change the brush color:

   - Set the line swatch on the Color tab. (See *Changing line and fill colors* on p. 225.)

     - or -

   - Click the **Color...** button on the context toolbar, and then choose your color from the **Color Picker** dialog. See *Using the Color Picker dialog* in online Help.

   Brush strokes cannot take a gradient fill. If applied, the base color of the fill is adopted.

4. To change brush stroke width:

   - Adjust the **Width** setting on the context toolbar (you can enter a value; click the up/down arrows; or click the right arrow and then drag the slider).

     - or -

At the bottom of the Line tab, drag the slider or enter a value in the adjacent box.

5. To adjust brush stroke opacity:

   ◉ Adjust the **Opacity** setting on the context toolbar. (100% opacity = no transparency; 0% opacity = fully transparent.)

   -or-

   ◉ On the Color tab, drag the **Transparency** slider to achieve the desired effect.

6. If, in step 1, you selected the **Brush** tool rather than an existing brush stroke, you'll see three additional options on the context toolbar: **Smoothness**, **Select-on-Create**, and **Fill-on-Create**.

   ◉ **Smoothness:** Adjust the degree of smoothing to be applied to the brush stroke by entering a value; clicking the up/down arrows; or clicking the right arrow and then dragging the slider.

   ◉ **Select-on-Create:** Click to enable or disable this option.

   Select-on-Create disabled:
   When you release the mouse button, the stroke you just created is not selected. This means that if you want to edit or add to the stroke, you must first select it. Use this method when you're happy to set all your brush stroke properties *before* painting—and particularly if you intend to paint repeatedly with the same brush stroke style.

Select-on-Create enabled:

When you release the mouse button, the curve or stroke you just created is automatically selected, allowing you to add to or edit it immediately. Use this method when you want to change your brush stroke properties (color, width, opacity, etc.) frequently.

Press the **Esc** key to deselect the current brush stroke.

Fill-on-Create: Enable this option if you want to fill the unclosed curve produced with a brush stroke with the fill color defined on the **Color** tab. (See *Changing line and fill colors* on p. 225.)

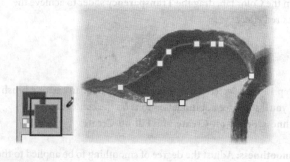

Working with
color

12

Changing fill and line color

You can apply colors to the outline and interior of closed shapes and text objects, and to lines and line segments.

In the **Digikit Browser**, the **Swatches** category offers a selection of colors specifically chosen to complement your installed Digikits. Once a Digikit is selected, these colors become available in the **Digikit** palette, which displays on the **Color** tab.

To apply fill and line color, you can:

- Select a swatch from the Digikit palette. (See below.)

- Apply a color tint or a transparent fill. (See below.)

- Use the Color tab's Color Picker to apply a color used elsewhere on your page. (See below.)

- Use the **Color** tab's Color Wheel, Color box, or sliders. (For more on the **Color** tab, see online Help.)

- Mix a custom color in the **Color Picker** dialog. (See *Using the Color Picker* in online Help.)

- Apply a gradient fill. (See *Applying gradient fills* on p. 228.)

- Apply a plasma or mesh fill. (See online Help.)

Applying colors from the Digikit palette

1. Select a shape, line, or text object.

2. On the **Color** tab:

 To change line color, click to select the **Line** swatch.

To change fill color, click to select the **Fill** swatch.

3. Click a palette swatch. The color is applied and the **Line/Fill** swatch updates with the selected color.

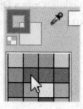

For information on switching palettes, see *Using color palettes* on p. 238.

Applying color tints

1. Select a shape, line, or text object.

2. On the **Color** tab:

    ○ Click to select the **Line** or **Fill** swatch, as described in step 2 above.

    ○ In the Color Mode drop-down list, select **Tinting**.

3. Drag the [slider] slider to the right to lighten the tint, or to the left to darken the tint.

    You can also enter a percentage value in the box (0% resets to the original color).

Applying transparent fills

1. Select a shape, line, or text object.

2. On the **Color** tab, click to select the **Line** or **Fill** swatch, as described above.

3. On the **Color** tab, click the 🔲 **No Fill** swatch.

> This applies transparency to items with line/fill properties, such as shapes and text. For pictures, clicking this swatch resets the original colors. See also *Applying transparency* on p. 155.

Applying colors with the Color Picker

1. Select a shape, line, or text object.

2. On the **Color** tab:

   - Click to select the **Line** or **Fill** swatch, as described above.

   - Click the 🖌 **Color Picker**.

3. On your page, click on your chosen pickup color with the pickup cursor (to magnify the color swatch, hold down the mouse button).

4. The color is picked up and displayed in the 🖌🔲 **Picked Color** swatch.

5. On the **Color** tab, click the **Picked Color** swatch to apply the color.

6. **Optional:** To add the color to your **Document** palette, click the ▷ **Color Tab Menu** button and select **Add to palette**. (See also *Using color palettes* on p. 238.)

Applying gradient fills

Gradient fills include the **Linear**, **Radial**, **Ellipse**, **Conical**, **Square**, **Three Color**, and **Four Color** types. All of these apply color 'spectrums' in a **fill path** spreading between two or more **nodes**. Once you've applied a gradient fill, you can edit its fill path and change its colors.

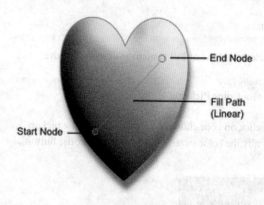

End Node

Fill Path
(Linear)

Start Node

Applying a gradient fill

1. Select an item on your page.

2. Click the **Fill Tool**.

3. Click and drag on the item to define the fill path. The item takes a simple **Linear** fill, grading from the current color of the item, ending in white (items filled with white will grade from white to black, to show contrast).

💡 To constrain the fill path in 15° increments, hold down the **Shift** key while dragging.

4. Optional: To change the fill type, choose from the drop-down list on the Fill context toolbar.

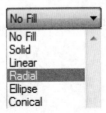

The new fill path displays. Note that this will differ depending on the fill type selected.

Editing a gradient fill path

1. Select an item with a gradient fill applied.

2. Click the 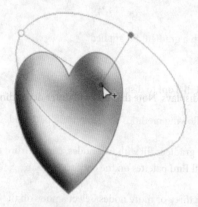 **Fill Tool** to display the fill path.

3. Move the fill path nodes by clicking and dragging them.

- or -

Click and drag across the item to define a new fill path.

💡 To constrain the fill path in 15° increments, hold down the **Shift** key while dragging.

💡 To ensure that the origin of the gradient remains at the item's center point, hold down the **Ctrl** key while dragging.

Adding and deleting fill path nodes

1. Select an item with a gradient fill applied.

2. Click the **Fill Tool** to display the fill path.

3. To add a node, click anywhere on the fill path.

   - or -

   To delete a node, click to select it and then press the **Delete** key.

See also *Editing gradient fills* on p. 232.

Changing node colors

1. Select an item with a gradient fill applied.

2. Click the **Fill Tool** to display the fill path.

3. Use any of the following methods to recolour fill path nodes:

   ○ For a simple gradient fill with two nodes, choose from the **Fill Start** and **Fill End** palettes on the context toolbar.

   ○ For fills with three or more nodes, select a node on the fill path, and then choose from the **Fill Color** palette on the context toolbar.

Select a node and then on the **Color** tab, click a color swatch. See *Editing gradient fills* below.

 Right-click the filled item and choose **Format>Fill...** (or choose the command from the **Format** menu).

Use the **Gradient Fill Editor** to add/remove nodes, modify node colors and alter node positions along the path. See *Editing gradient fills* below.

> Adjustment techniques, Fill Tool, and context toolbar options differ depending on the fill type.

Editing gradient fills

You can edit a gradient fill spectrum directly, using the **Fill Tool**, or you can use the **Gradient Fill Editor**. Both methods let you define **key color**s, with a spread of hues between each, to create a "spectrum" effect.

While the **Fill Tool** method is quick and easy, the **Gradient Fill Editor** also lets you fine-tune the actual spread of color between key colors.

Editing gradient fills with the Fill Tool

1. Select the filled item and then click the **Fill Tool** to display the fill path.

2. Nodes mark the key colors of the color spread(s).

 To add a key color:
Drag a color swatch from the **Color** tab's palette onto a portion of

the fill path where there is no node. A new node appears.

Note: Be sure the tip of the pointer is directly over the fill path when you release the mouse button (watch the cursor). If it's not, the color will be applied to the whole item as a solid fill.

⦿ **To change a key color:**

Click its node, and then click a color swatch on the **Color** tab's palette.

-or-

Drag from a color swatch onto any node. (You don't need to select the node first.)

⦿ **To move a key color** (except the end colors):
Use the **Fill Tool** to drag its node to a new position along the fill path.

⦿ **To delete a key color** (except the end colors):
Select its node and press the **Delete** key.

Editing gradient fills using the Gradient Fill Editor

1. Select the filled item, click the **Fill Tool**, and then click **Fill Style** on the context toolbar.

    -or-

    Right-click the filled item and click **Format>Fill...** (or choose the command from the **Format** menu).

2. The **Gradient Fill Editor** dialog displays the gradient spectrum, with markers indicating the key colors of the color spread(s).

    In this example, the gradient has just one spread, between blue and yellow key colors. The fill path's **start node** appears at the left, and its **end node** at the right.

To change a key color:

*   Click its marker (selected markers have black arrows), click the

     Color button, and then choose from the displayed
    palette of colors.

    - or -

● To change a key color to one that already exists in the spectrum, click its marker, and then click on the spectrum with the dropper.

In our example, we've changed the leftmost key color to orange.

To add a key color:

● Click just below the spectrum (you'll see a hand cursor) where you want to place the new key color.

A new marker appears, using black as the default key color. (Note that the new marker's arrow is black, indicating that it's selected.)

You can now edit the color of the new marker, as described in the previous step.

In the following example, we've changed the new key color to red. The marker shows the new key color, and is still selected.

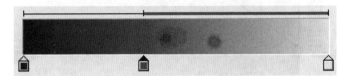

To move a key color (except the end colors):

- Drag its marker to a new position along the spectrum.

  - or -

  In the **Node** box, type a value to specify the marker's position as a
  percentage along the spectrum (for example, you could set equally
  spaced pointers at 25, 50, and 75).

To delete a key color (except the end colors):

- Select its marker and click **Delete**. (**Note:** Key color deletion is not
  reversible using the **Undo** command.)

Adjusting gradient fill color spreads

In the **Gradient Fill Editor**, the red bar above the gradient spectrum shows
which section of the gradient is currently selected (always to the right of the
selected key color marker).

The diagonal **color contour line** lets you adjust the spread of colors between
pairs of key colors, and shows the distribution of colors along the selected
gradient section.

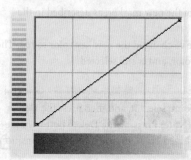

Initially, the contour appears as a straight line because colors are graduated evenly from one key color to the next. By changing the shape of the contour, you can change this color distribution along the selected section of the gradient.

To adjust the contour:

1. To extend one key color or the other, and vary the rate of transition, click and drag on the contour line.

   - or -

   To apply a preset color contour, select from the drop-down list. (The straight-line preset restores original settings.)

2. Optional:

   ● To add a new transition point, simply click on the line.

   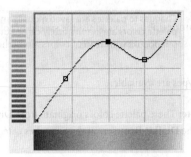

   ● To delete a transition point, select it, and then press the **Delete** key on your keyboard. (**Note:** Pressing the **Delete** button in the dialog will delete the selected gradient marker, not the transition point.)

- To straighten the line segments between transition points, select the **Straight graph** check box.

- To apply a tint to the fill, adjust the value in the **Fill tint** box.

3. Click **OK** to accept changes, or **Cancel** to abandon changes.

Using color palettes

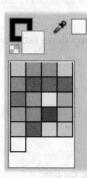

When you apply a **solid fill** or **line color**, you choose a color belonging to a color **palette**.

Only one palette can be active at any one time. The currently active palette is displayed as a gallery of swatches on the **Color** tab.

You can add, edit, and remove palette colors, and switch between different palettes at any time. You can also create your own custom palettes. (See *Creating custom palettes* in online Help.)

 Changes to palettes are saved globally and the new palette colors are automatically carried over to any new scrapbooks you create.

The following palette types are available:

- **Digikit palette:** These palette colors originate from Digikits—you'll see them in the **Digikit Browser**, in the **Swatches** category.

  If you choose **Start with a theme** from the **Startup Wizard**, the selected Digikit's palette is loaded by default and displayed on the **Color** tab. You can make changes to your **Digikit palette** (see below for details).

- **Document palette:** If you start a scrapbook from scratch, rather than from a Digikit, the default **Document** palette is displayed on the **Color** tab. This palette provides a set of commonly-used colors from which to choose.

You can edit the colors displayed in the **Document** palette—for example, you may want to add swatches from a Digikit or a themed palette, or add a color you have mixed yourself on the Color tab or Color Picker dialog. You can also save your **Document** palette for use in other scrapbooks.

- **Standard RGB** and **Standard CMYK palettes:** Palettes based on industry-standard color models.

- **Themed palettes:** Digital Scrapbook Artist also provides a range of designer-created themed palettes containing colors designed to work well together on the page.

When you save a scrapbook, its palette is saved along with it.

Switching palettes

1. On the **Color** tab, click **More...**

2. In the **Color Palette Designer**, the **Palettes** drop-down list displays all of the palettes installed with Digital Scrapbook Artist.

   Click the palette you want to use.

   The selected palette's colors appear as swatches in the **Color Palette Designer** and on the **Color** tab, replacing the swatches previously visible.

Adding swatches to the Digikit palette

1. On the context toolbar, click **Add items from Digikits**.

2. In Digikit Browser, click the **Browse my items** tab.

3. In the category list on the left, click **Swatches**.

4. Swatches already added to your **Digikit** palette are highlighted in the main window.

⊿ Doll House			Add all items ✓
H=1 S=60 L=85	H=330 S=16 L=68	H=23 S=26 L=65	H=61 S=41 L=75
H=54 S=24 L=55	H=356 S=72 L=55	H=356 S=30 L=53	H=19 S=44 L=47
H=155 S=22 L=50	H=87 S=34 L=62	H=38 S=81 L=91	H=35 S=42 L=69
H=43 S=43 L=61	H=72 S=29 L=54	H=280 S=9 L=35	H=16 S=66 L=75
H=22 S=67 L=78	H=3 S=23 L=47	H=41 S=42 L=82	H=39 S=19 L=80
H=0 S=0 L=100			

5. You can remove colors from the palette, and add colors from other installed Digikits.

   ● To remove a color from the palette, click to deselect it.

   ● To add a color, click to select it.

6. Click **Done**. Colors are automatically removed from/added to the **Digikit** palette displayed on the **Color** tab.

7. **Optional:**

   ● To add the color to your **Document** palette, click the ▷ **Color Tab Menu** button and choose **Add to Palette**.

      (You would do this if you intended to save your **Document** palette for use in other scrapbooks, for example.)

   ● To add the new color swatch to your Digikit, open **Digikit Creator** and save your Digikit. (See *Saving Digikits* on p. 66.)

   (See also *Editing palettes* on p. 241.)

Changing Document palette colors

You can add colors manually from the Color tab, or take them directly from an item's fill. Once a color is stored in the **Document** palette, you can edit it in the **Color Picker** dialog.

To add a color from an item's fill to the Document palette:

● Select an item that has a fill color you want to add to your palette, then click the ▷ **Color Tab Menu** button and select **Add to palette**.

To add a color manually from the Color tab:

1. On the **Color** tab:

   ● Click the **Fill** swatch, and then click to select your preferred color.

   -or-

   ● Click the 🖉 **Color Picker**, hold down the mouse button, and then click anywhere in your workspace to pick up your new color.

   Click the 🖉▢ **Picked Color** swatch to transfer the color to the **Fill** swatch.

2. Click the ▷ **Color Tab Menu** button and select **Add to palette**.

Editing palettes

To add a new palette swatch:

1. On the **Color** tab, right-click on the palette and click **Add**.

2. In the **Color Picker** dialog, choose your new color and click **OK**. (See *Using the Color Picker dialog* in online Help.)

   The color is added to the currently loaded palette.

3. **Optional:** To add the color to your **Document** palette, click the ▷ **Color Tab Menu** button and choose **Add to Palette**.

   (You would do this if you wanted to save your **Document** palette for use in other scrapbooks, for example.)

To edit a palette swatch:

1. On the **Color** tab, right-click on the swatch you want to edit and click **Edit**.

2. Follow step 2 above.

To remove a palette swatch:

● On the **Color** tab, right-click on the swatch you want to remove and click **Delete**.

Saving palettes

To save the currently active palette (the palette displayed on the Color tab):

1. On the **Color** tab, right-click the palette and select **Palette Manager**.

2. In the **Palette Manager** dialog, click the **Options** button, and select **Save Palette As**.

3. Save the palette to a new *.plt file.

To save a different palette:

1. On the **Color** tab, click **More...**

2. In the **Color Palette Designer**, in the **Palettes** drop-down list, select the palette you want to save.

3. Click **Save**.

4. Save the palette to a new *.plt file.

By default, palette files are saved to the **Palettes** folder of your installation directory.

If you store your palette to a different location, it will not appear in the **Palettes** drop-down list. To use a palette that is not saved in the **Palettes** folder, you need to load it.

Loading other palettes

In the **Color Palette Designer** the drop-down **Palettes** list lets you quickly switch to any of the palettes saved in the **Palettes** folder. However, you can also load palettes that are stored elsewhere on your computer.

To load a palette:

1.   On the **Color** tab, click **More...**

2.   In the **Color Palette Designer**, click **Load**.

3.   Navigate to and select the palette you want to load.

4.   Click **Open**.

     The loaded palette's colors appear as swatches in the **Color Palette Designer** and on the **Color** tab, replacing the swatches previously visible.

Arranging items

13

Rotating and shearing items

Rotating items

1. Select the item(s) with the ![Select tool cursor] **Select** tool.

2. Hover over the rotate handle, when you see the cursor change, drag in the direction in which you want to rotate the item.

   As you drag, the angle of rotation is temporarily displayed around the item's origin point (shown as ⦿). This temporary display of information is known as **tool feedback**.

- To rotate in 15° intervals, press and hold down the **Shift** key while dragging.

- To undo the rotation, double-click the rotate handle.

To change the rotation origin point:

1. Click and drag the origin point to any position on the page. (This can be outside the item itself—useful for rotating grouped items around a central point.)

2. Drag the repositioned rotate handle. The item rotates about the new origin point.

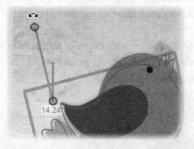

 Additional rotation options are provided on the **Arrange** and **Transform** tabs, and on the **Arrange** menu. For details, see online Help.

Shearing items

1. Select the item(s) with the **Select** tool.

2. Hover over a center edge handle.

When you see the Shear cursor, click and drag in the direction in which you want to shear the item, and then release.

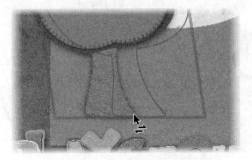

- To copy and shear an item, press and hold down the **Ctrl** key while dragging—this preserves the original item, while shearing the new copied item as you drag.

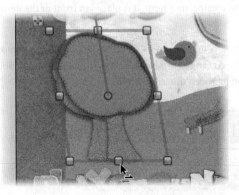

- For precise shearing, enter an exact **Shear** value in the Transform tab.

Ordering items

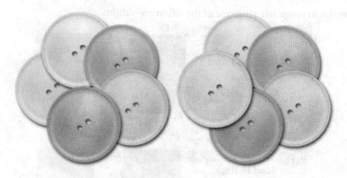

The items on your scrapbook page are 'stacked' on top of each other, the front-most item (e.g., blue button above) being the one on top of the stack (also known as **Z-order**).

Each time you create a new item, it is placed in front of the items already there.

You can move any item to any position in the ordering sequence using buttons on the **Arrange** tab, shown below. In the illustration above, the yellow button has been moved from the back to the front.

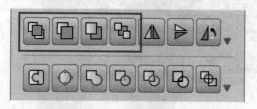

 Equivalent commands are available from the **Arrange** menu's **Order** items submenu.

To change an item's position:

On the **Arrange** tab, click one of the following buttons:

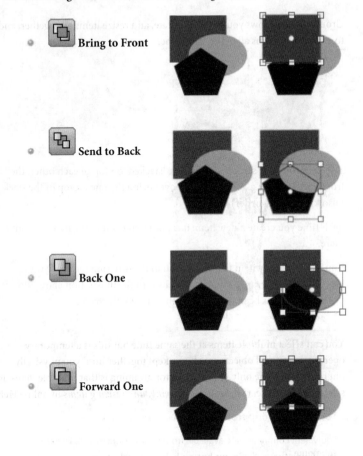

- **Bring to Front**
- **Send to Back**
- **Back One**
- **Forward One**

 Don't confuse the concept of item ordering with that of page layers. (See *Working with layers* in online Help.)

Grouping items

Grouping items prevents you from accidentally altering them.

Grouping also allows you to move, rotate, and resize items all together, and to edit similar items all at the same time.

Ungroup

You can select multiple items at the same time but this is a temporary operation; grouped objects are always kept together until you physically ungroup them. The only requirement for grouping is that multiple items are selected in advance. (See *Selecting, moving, and resizing items* in online Help.)

To create a group from a multiple selection:

- Click the **Group** button below the selection.

To ungroup (turn a group back into a multiple selection):

- Click the **Ungroup** button below the selection.

In general, any operation you carry out on a group affects each member of the group. For example, property changes applied to a group—such as changing line or fill—will affect all the items contained in the group.

You can select and edit items within groups, without having to ungroup them.

To select an individual item within a group:

- Press and hold down the **Ctrl** key and then click on the item. The item is selected and can be edited.

- To deselect the item and its group, click elsewhere on the page.

Sharing and
publishing

Sharing via website

You can share your scrapbook by print, via email, as a distributable electronic PDF, or via the **www.daisytrail.com** website.

Publishing to DaisyTrail lets you contribute to the growing collection of published scrapbooks, and share your scrapbook with friends, family, and like-minded scrapbookers!

To share your scrapbooks via website, simply complete the following steps:

- Register on the website.

- Set up account information in Digital Scrapbook Artist.

- Upload your chosen scrapbook.

The **www.daisytrail.com** website is designed specifically as a scrapbook community. Main website features include:

- **Scrapbook rating**
  Rate and comment on other people's scrapbooks—and have your own scrapbook assessed by the community. Click the **I love it!** voting button to award your favorite scrapbooks.

- **Work in groups**
  Create groups of users with similar interests—great for schools, clubs, or maybe just your network of scrapbooking friends. Use the **Group Wall** to view published scrapbooks in a chosen group, which can be private, public or 'friends only.' Post to **group forums** restricted to just group members.

- **Search**
  Find scrapbooks, groups, or other scrapbookers throughout the website.

- **Make new friends!**
  Social networking meets scrapbooking! Use **email** or user discussion **forums** to build friendships with other scrapbookers, especially those you add to your friends list. Even upload photos of yourself!

- **Profile management**
  Manage your tagline, password, timezone, language, and email notifications.

- **Free stuff**
  Each month **daisytrail.com** will give away a new free Digikit or font for you to download.

- **DaisyTrail shop**
  Buy and download **individual themed Digikits**—or buy **Digikit Collections** on DVD. You can also buy **Font Collections**, plus a selection of other goodies.

Registering

1. Click **DaisyTrail Upload** on the **Standard** toolbar.

2. If you've not registered before, click the **Join Now!** button. You'll be taken directly to **www.daisytrail.com** registration.

3. From the registration form, enter your personal information, including an email address to which an activation message will be sent. If you need **Help**, use the link provided.

4. Click **Create Account**. For account activation, you'll need to check your email and click on the activation message sent to you. This may take time depending on your ISP and connection.

 Remember your Username and Password. You'll need to re-enter this information into Digital Scrapbook Artist.

5. Registration is complete after activation.

   All you need to do now is enter your account details into your Digital Scrapbook Artist program.

   If you've already registered but not added your account details, click **Login**. This takes you to your account details where you can enter details as described in the following section.

If you don't add your DaisyTrail user account details, you'll be reminded to do so every eight days. You can register on the website, then transfer your username and password over, or cancel to enter your details later.

Setting up account details in Digital Scrapbook Artist

1. Select **Options...** on the **Tools** menu.

2. In the **Upload** pane, enter your **Username** and **Password**.

3. (Optional) Click the **Test** button to verify that the account details are correct. If successful, a "*Username and password valid*" message displays.

    If you've forgotten your password or you've not already registered, use the accompanying **Reset Password** and **Register** buttons. For the latter, you'll be directed to the **Registration** page on the website. Complete the registration details and click **Create Account**.

4. (Optional) Reduce the upload **Quality** to 96 DPI to speed up file transfer if your Internet connection is 56k dial-up modem (at the expense of zoom quality).

    Otherwise, use the default 300 DPI for broadband and all other faster Internet connections.

 If you change your account details on the website at a later date, you'll also need to make these account changes in Digital Scrapbook Artist.

Uploading

Once you've successfully created your account you can upload your scrapbook, with the option of including only specific or all pages.

☑ Page 1   ☑ Page 2   ☑ Page 3

To upload your scrapbook:

1. Click **DaisyTrail Upload** on the **Standard** toolbar.

2. In the dialog, uncheck pages you don't want to upload (use the scroll bar to view all pages).

3. (Optional) For the upload you can choose a different account to upload to. Enter a different **Username** and **Password**.

4. Click **Upload** to transfer your selected pages.

5. On upload, a progress bar indicates upload status.

   On completion, click **OK** to close the dialog or click **View** to immediately see your uploaded scrapbook on the website.

Basic printing

Digital Scrapbook Artist supports printing directly to a physical printer (e.g., All-in-ones, Inkjet and Laser printers), with options for scaling and thumbnail printing.

To print:

1. Click **File>Print...** (or right-click on the page or pasteboard area and click **Print**).

2. In the **Print** dialog, select the number of pages to print, and optionally a **Print Size** (as original document, scaled, or as thumbnails).

3. Click **Print**.

Exporting as PDF

The cross-platform **Adobe PDF** file format is a worldwide standard for document distribution, which works equally well for electronic or paper publishing. It excels as an electronic distribution medium as it is device- and platform-independent.

To make scrapbook sharing easy, you can export your scrapbook as a PDF file (Acrobat 4.0 compatible). In doing so, all your scrapbook's colors will be output in an RGB color space, and all scrapbook pages will be rasterized (converted to bitmaps) on export.

Exporting as a PDF file

1. Click **File>Export>Export as PDF...**

2. In the dialog, select a **Print Range**:

   - **Entire Scrapbook**: Exports the whole scrapbook.

   - **Current page**: Exports only the page currently displayed.

   - **Pages**: Enter a page range (e.g., 3-5) to export a limited selection of pages (or individual page numbers, if separated by commas). If you've set a range, you can further export just odd or even pages in the range from the drop-down list.

3. (Optional) Set various options as follows:

- For more convenient on-screen viewing in Adobe Reader, specify how your scrapbook will initially appear by selecting the **Fit to complete page** or **Fit to page width** check box.

- By default, your PDF file will display in your currently installed Adobe Reader immediately after export finishes. If you do not want to preview your file immediately after export, clear the **Preview PDF file** check box.

- Select a **Print Quality** level from the drop-down list. **Best** quality offers 300 dpi lossless export (no compression). Other list options offer lower resolution export, with smaller file sizes offered as quality decreases.

4. Click **OK** to proceed with the export.

5. Choose a location and file name for your PDF file. Click **Save**.

Once export completes, the PDF displays if **Preview PDF file** was selected in step 3 above.

Index

15

Notes

Notes

Notes

Notes

Notes

Notes

Notes